preserving communities & corridors

DEFENDERS OF WILDLIFE

1244 NINETEENTH STREET, NW

WASHINGTON, DC 20036

CONTENTS

Overview from Defenders' President

By M. Rupert Cutler

Our society seems to learn ecological principles very slowly—too slowly, obviously, to benefit the plant and animal species that have recently become extinct. Could their loss also be accounted for by mankind's lack of a wildlife ethic?

On behalf of all the remaining species—including *Homo sapiens*—it behooves us to accelerate that learning process. And when an opportunity arises to adopt an important new tool to prevent species endangerment, we should waste no time in taking advantage of it.

There does seem to be something new under the sun, as far as practical means of conserving biological diversity are concerned. That approach—the conscious preservation of migration corridors or land bridges between fragmented centers of plant and animal species richness—is what this book is intended, in part, to describe and advocate.

Not that this technique is radically different from nature-preserving recommendations made in the past. But its advantages as a specific prescription—and as an alternative to setting aside disconnected bits of habitat here and there—have become more obvious as our once-extensive undeveloped forests, grasslands, and wetlands have become more fragmented.

George Perkins Marsh, in his landmark book *Man and Nature* (1864), warned us more than four generations ago not to "derange and destroy" arrangements of nature:

> In countries untrodden by man, the . . . distribution of vegetable and animal life [is] subject to change only from geological influences so slow in their operation that the geographical conditions may be regarded as constant and immutable. These arrangements of nature it is, in most cases, highly desirable substantially to maintain, when such regions become the seat of organized commonwealths. It is, therefore, a matter of the first importance, that, in commencing the process of fitting them for a permanent civilized occupation, the transforming operations should be so conducted as not unnecessarily to derange and destroy what, in too many cases, it is beyond the power of man to rectify or restore.

Aldo Leopold rediscovered this land management principle one generation ago, summarizing it in his 1953 essay "Conservation":

> The outstanding scientific discovery of the twentieth century is not television or radio, but rather the complexity of the land organism. Only those who know the most about

it can appreciate how little we know about it. The last word in ignorance is the man who says of an animal or plant: "What good is it?" If the land mechanism as a whole is good, then every part is good, whether we understand it or not. If the biota, in the course of aeons, has built something we like but do not understand, then who but a fool would discard seemingly useless parts? To keep every cog and wheel is the first precaution of intelligent tinkering.

Don't "derange and destroy." "Keep every cog and wheel." The pleas of Marsh and Leopold for the preservation of biological diversity seem practically modern.

The connection between ethics and wildlife habitat conservation was made by Leopold (1949):

> There is as yet no ethic dealing with man's relation to land and to the animals and plants which grow upon it. Land, like Odysseus' slave-girls, is still property. The land-relation is still strictly economic, entailing privileges but not obligations. The extension of ethics to this . . . element in human environment is, if I read the evidence correctly, an evolutionary possibility and an ecological necessity.

Aldo Leopold (1949) tacitly suggested the need to protect and link wildlife habitats as a practical means to the ethical end of defending wildlife when he observed:

> The National Parks do not suffice as a means of perpetuating the larger carnivores; witness the precarious status of the grizzly bear, and the fact that the park system is already wolfless. . . . The parks are certainly too small for such a far-ranging species as the wolf. Many animal species, for reasons unknown, do not seem to thrive as detached islands of population.
>
> The most feasible way to enlarge the area available for wilderness fauna is for the wilder parts of the National Forests, which usually surround the Parks, to function as parks in respect to threatened species. . . . Saving the grizzly requires a *series* of large areas from which roads and livestock are

Leopold showed the way by expanding our vision of the role of the wildlife biologist to encompass saving a series of large habitats and encouraging the greatest possible diversity by linking these habitats.

excluded, or in which livestock damage is compensated. . . [emphasis added].

In her 1974 biography of Leopold, Susan Flader concludes:

> Three decades of experience trying to "control" wildlife populations by manipulating selected environmental factors had had a profoundly sobering effect on Leopold. A proper function of management, it now became apparent to him, was to encourage the greatest possible diversity in an attempt to preserve the widest possible realm in which natural processes might seek their own equilibrium.

Keep every cog and wheel. Provide a series of large areas from which roads and livestock are excluded. Leopold may not have used today's terms "corridor," "land bridge," or "greenway." But he showed the way by expanding our vision of the role of the wildlife biologist to encompass saving a series of large habitats and encouraging the greatest possible diversity by linking these habitats.

Which brings us to today's problems and opportunities. The time is right, it seems to us at Defenders of Wildlife, to win political support for the universal application of the wildlife habitat-connection approach to the protection of biological diversity.

A common thread runs through the following two quotations from widely disparate sources. The first is from the 1987 report of the President's Commission on Americans Outdoors:

> We recommend [that] communities establish Greenways, corridors of private and public recreation lands and waters, to provide people with access to open spaces and to link together the rural and urban spaces in the American landscape.
>
> Greenways connect new and existing recreation and conservation areas, like parks and forests and refuges, and corridors to link them together.
>
> [Greenways] have the potential to be this country's most important land-based effort for conservation and recreation in the next several decades.

The second is from a 1988 paper entitled "Beyond Endangered Species: An Integrated Strategy for the Preservation of Biological Diversity," by conservation biologists J. Michael Scott, Blair Csuti, and others:

> We can continue focusing our efforts on the critically endangered through a species approach. . . . Or, we can proceed in a more positive direction by shifting some of our focus to a more broad-based ecosystem approach aimed at preventing species from becoming endangered. . . .
>
> We believe that a useful approach to developing a long-range strategy for preserving biological diversity is a multi-faceted analysis of the gaps in the network of protected areas. . . . Questions addressed in the analysis would include[,] Do adequate landscape corridors exist between areas of high species richness to provide for dispersal and interbreeding of populations?

The common thread is the use of the term "corridors." Whether they refer to "parks and forests and refuges" or "areas of high species richness," both prescriptions call for the conscious dedication of landscape corridors to link vital wildlife habitats.

Defenders of Wildlife hopes to be able to assist the political and nongovernment organization leaders who produced the President's Commission report and the conservation biologists who wrote

The time is right to win political support for the wildlife habitat-connection approach to the preservation of biological diversity.

"Beyond Endangered Species" to reinforce each other's conclusions, to the end that the corridors of which they both speak will be protected and many plant and animal species thereby will be prevented from becoming endangered.

This publication, *In Defense of Wildlife: Preserving Communities and Corridors*, represents the first of several steps Defenders is taking in a campaign to win recognition of and support for the concept of linking major habitat fragments by means of dedicated corridors. The first paper, by Larry D. Harris—author of the award-winning book *Fragmented Forests* and professor at the University of Florida—and Peter B. Gallagher, makes the case for the preservation of wildlife movement corridors, riparian and otherwise, to connect in a national network the fragmented habitats of the United States. Professor Harris also provides here an extensive bibliography that we believe is the first published compilation of the major sources documenting the need for preserving biological diversity through protecting key habitats joined by corridors. The second paper, by Aubrey Stephen Johnson, Defenders' regional representative for Arizona and New Mexico, focuses on the particular importance of protecting and restoring riparian corridors in the desert Southwest to prevent further endangerment of species.

This volume also includes a detailed account by Ginger Merchant Meese, Defenders' Washington, D.C. representative for endangered species, of the current status of work to implement the Endangered Species Act, together with a description of the amendments to that statute when it was reauthorized in 1988 and recommendations on how the act can be used more effectively as one tool in preserving biological diversity. Albert M. Manville II, Defenders' senior staff wildlife biologist, describes in his paper the history and current status of the 1980 Fish and Wildlife Conservation Act (the "Nongame Act"), designed to provide grant support to the states for programs that would enhance their efforts to protect all native wildlife—but yet to be funded. The final report, by Sara Vickerman, regional program director for Defenders of Wildlife, builds on original survey data from all 50 state wildlife agencies to assess their efforts in behalf of those species known to wildlife biologists as "nongame" and to the general public as "watchable wildlife."

Our intention here is to report on and applaud the efforts of federal and state wildlife agencies to save all wildlife species, while giving special attention to their efforts to protect diverse habitats. By publicizing the need to identify and protect large remnants of every native plant and animal community, Defenders hopes to win more widespread appreciation of the fact that only through effective habitat conservation can endangerment be prevented and biological diversity be perpetuated.

The concept of habitat conservation to foster recovery of endangered species as well as to fend off endangerment is not new. But the concept of preserving strips of land and water connecting species-rich examples of high-quality habitat such as parks and wildernesses—or even connecting ungrazed farm woodlots by means of hedgerows—to enable species to move from one habitat to another is relatively new, at least to nonbiologists.

That single concept—the notion that links between the remaining islands of our fragmented forests and other key wildlife habitats must be preserved if many species are to survive—is the special focus of this book. Call them greenways, land bridges, travel lanes, or landscape linkages, the prompt identification and protection of wildlife movement corridors may spell the difference between survival and extinction for such diverse species as the spotted owl and the Florida panther.

The protected-corridor concept is as important in the Corn Belt (to permit fox, river otter, and mink to move undetected from one block of woods or marsh to another) as it is in the Alps-like North

*O*nly through effective habitat conservation can endangerment be prevented and biological diversity be perpetuated.

Cascades (for the gray wolf and grizzly bear) and the Mississippi Delta (for the Louisiana black bear). It can be applied on private as well as public land.

Billions of dollars are going each year to farmers to encourage them to leave parts of their farms untilled to reduce crop surpluses, increase crop prices, and save topsoil. Perhaps participating farmers would be willing, in exchange, to leave streamside vegetation on their properties intact for wildlife habitat and other greenway-related public benefits. Industrial and nonindustrial private forest landowners should be eligible for property tax relief and other incentives in exchange for easements across their land for wildlife travel corridors.

This set of reports is intended to reflect Defenders' conclusion that the single-species approach to the problem of endangerment—the use of most of the resources available to try to bring a handful of highly visible species back from the very brink of extinction, often through captive breeding—should give way to or at least be complemented over time by a multi-species approach based on the preservation of endangered habitats with their animal and plant communities intact.

Each intact habitat or ecosystem represents a community of hundreds of plant and animal species. Its protection will help assure the perpetuation of batches of species, some of which may be unknown as yet to science. By preventing species endangerment, this proactive approach may reduce the need for the expensive, frustrating, last-ditch, and in the end often fruitless campaigns that have been waged to save the last few individuals of a relict species such as the dusky seaside sparrow or the California condor.

Defenders of Wildlife will continue to publicize the need to protect wildlife habitat gaps and corridors and to win adoption of this new land acquisition criterion and management planning goal. This effort represents the natural evolution of Defenders' long-standing program to prevent the endangerment of such wide-ranging carnivores as the red and gray wolves, the grizzly bear, and the mountain lion. It comes at a time when the attention of policy-makers has been drawn to the transnational, interconnected nature of natural resources conservation problems in general and threats to biological diversity in particular.

The emphasis on corridor protection provides a natural link between Defenders' traditional interests in the welfare of mammalian and avian predators and two themes now on the agendas of many private and public agencies: the preservation of biological diversity around the world and the creation of a national system of dedicated greenways linking American communities from coast to coast.

Far more Americans now relate to wildlife as "nonconsumers"—as birders, photographers, hikers, students, teachers, and scientists—than as "consumers"—as hunters, fishermen, and trappers. The mandate given our public wildlife agencies is to protect our wildlife species in all their wonderful diversity for all the people and to prevent the loss of species.

Taken literally, this broad mandate opens doors for wildlife agencies to a much larger constituency than they have directed their programs toward in the past. In many states there has been a decline of interest in hunting and an accompanying drop in license-sales revenue while there has been a steep increase in the number of citizens visiting wildlife areas armed with binoculars and cameras. An awkward courtship is underway between the wildlife agencies and the nonconsumptive users of wildlife. Mutually supportive relationships have been established in many states, to the credit of those involved.

Hunters traditionally have organized effectively and have been willing to pay, through license fees and excise taxes on their equipment, for management programs that suppress some species (notably predators) to create artificially high numbers of others—a few favored game species, such as the white-tailed deer and the exotic ring-necked pheasant. Habitat manipulation to increase game species populations, such as wetlands creation for waterfowl, may help nongame species as well. However, extensive forest clear-cuts for deer, the flooding of marshes for ducks or fish, and other habitat alterations can result in the loss of less abundant or less popular species.

Defenders will encourage all of the agencies whose mission it is to maintain a state's or the nation's wildlife resources to accept as their overriding goal the perpetuation of the biological diversity found within their jurisdictions. We will encourage these agencies to provide a variety of areas and programs responsive to each of the groups whose special interest is wildlife—sportsmen, birders, photographers, families who seek convenient access to wildlife viewing sites, scientists who require protected research natural areas, teachers who need outdoor laboratories in which to teach ecology, and others.

The agencies' overriding responsibility, however, is to see to it that viable examples of all of our native plant and animal communities—"every cog and wheel"—are protected or restored for future generations to cherish and enjoy.

He who pays the piper calls the tune. That is why our nation's wildlife programs to date have emphasized game species abundance and the enhancement of hunting and fishing opportunities. As more Americans who do not hunt or fish but devote their leisure time to wildlife-related outdoor pursuits let their preference for more comprehensive public wildlife management programs responsive to their interests be known and as means are provided for these nonconsumptive users of wildlife to pay their way, our public wildlife programs will evolve in that direction.

Defenders of Wildlife will strive to be the constructive voice of that growing nonconsumptive-user constituency. And the protection of essential habitats and wildlife movement corridors will be a key plank in our platform of recommended wildlife conservation practices.

The extension of ethics to man's relationship with wildlife is an ecological necessity. And, as the reports that follow show, there is no more practical way to perpetuate our wildlife legacy—and thus to fulfill the obligations that go with the privileges of being human—than by preserving and connecting the rich diversity of native plant and animal communities.

Readers' comments and suggestions are welcome.

M. Rupert Cutler was appointed president of Defenders of Wildlife in 1987. He holds a Ph.D. degree in resource development from Michigan State University, where he taught environmental policy. Dr. Cutler served as assistant secretary of agriculture for conservation, research and education, U.S. Department of Agriculture, during the Carter administration. In that capacity he oversaw the drafting of National Forest planning regulations and initiated the second Forest Service Roadless Area Review and Evaluation (RARE II).

Selected Bibliography

Flader, S.L. 1974. Thinking like a mountain. University of Nebraska Press, Lincoln, Nebraska.

Leopold, A. 1949. A Sand County almanac. Oxford University Press, New York.

_____. 1953. Round River. Oxford University Press, New York.

Marsh, G.P. 1864. Man and nature. John Harvard Library Edition, 1965. Harvard University Press, Cambridge.

President's Commission on Americans Outdoors. 1987. Americans outdoors: The report of the President's Commission. Island Press, Washington, D.C.

Scott, J.M., B. Csuti, K. Smith, J.E. Estes, and S. Caicco. 1988. Beyond endangered species: An integrated strategy for the preservation of biological diversity. *Endangered Species Update* 5 (August): 43-48.

New Initiatives for Wildlife Conservation

By Larry D. Harris
and Peter B. Gallagher

The Need for Movement Corridors

In the spring of 1986, a 195-pound male black bear from Big Cypress National Preserve embarked on an astounding journey through southwestern Florida. Captured as a nuisance animal in a rural area, the bear was equipped with a radio collar, released where he was found, and recaptured 100 miles north of his former range.

For eleven weeks, this bear wandered more than 200 miles under the gaze of scientists. He traveled a northerly course through six counties, crossed eight major highways and nearly a dozen other roadways, swam the Caloosahatchee River, and crossed numerous canals, fences, and farmlands. As he moved along abandoned railroad tracks and skirted densely populated suburbs—even loitering and observing the fireworks near a large Fourth of July outdoor picnic—he negotiated bee yards, turkey pens, and numerous roadside garbage containers. Ultimately, he had to be recaptured by state wildlife personnel near Lake Placid.[1]

The young southern Florida male had moved about as we would expect any bear to do. He moved to find food; he moved to locate cover. As a young male, he may have been moving to emigrate—a difficult task considering the fragmented habitats of the eastern United States—or he may have moved to reproduce, to share southern Florida genetic material with an uncollared central Florida female bear he encountered just before he was removed from the wild. Forces yet to be understood by biologists stimulated the bear to move and he went, even though there was no logical path to follow.[2]

From what we know about animal mortality in Florida, the bear's trip was extremely dangerous. Since 1976, documented bear roadkills have risen steadily, particularly among dispersing males (see figure 1). Florida Department of Natural Resources biologist Walt Thomson notes, "State Road 46 is basically functioning as a wildlife killing machine."

This article is Journal Series Number 9668 of the Florida Agricultural Experiment Station, Gainesville, Florida.

There is little doubt that the same trip taken by this bear's ancestors in 1956 or even 1976 in a more forested and less peopled landscape would have exposed them to significantly less danger. [3]

This is not only a problem for bears. Roadkills are the number one known cause of death for all of Florida's remaining large mammals except white-tailed deer. Sixty-five percent of known Florida panther deaths since 1981 have been roadkills. Roadkill is the major cause of death for the endangered Key deer isolated on Big Pine Key and the American crocodile on the northern Keys. In the water, motorboat collisions have long been documented as the principal human-related mortality factor for manatees.

Radio-telemetry studies on bears, panthers, and numerous other species dramatically demonstrate the expansive tracts of habitat required for our resident wildlife to traverse their home ranges (see figure 2). Animals do not wait for the traffic signal to flash "Walk." Our refusal to incorporate movement corridors across human-dominated landscapes into our conservation strategies has made luck—enjoyed in great measure by this bear—the chief prerequisite for survival for much of Florida's wildlife. Sadly, given the interrupted landscapes and barriers to animal movement that increasingly dominate the eastern United States, it is extremely doubtful that any bear, panther, bobcat, mink, or otter—the low-density, top-of-the-foodchain, wide-movers—could ever duplicate our young Florida bear's recorded movement.

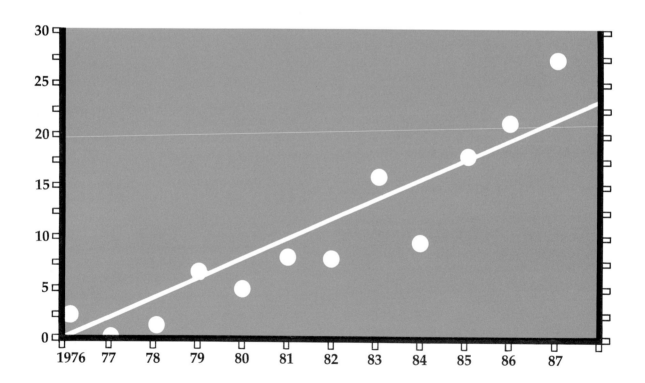

Figure 1. Black Bear Roadkills Collected in Florida, 1976-1987.

Vehicle collisions are the number one known cause of mortality for most of Florida's large mammal species, including bear, panther, Key deer, and manatee (boat collisions). Mortality increases as vehicle traffic increases. [1]

Figure 2. Approximate Ranging Areas in Acres for Otter, Bobcat, Black Bear, and Florida Panther.

Because the home range of individual animals of these species is large, they must traverse miles of hostile landscape riddled with roads and shopping centers. A male panther may range over 50 miles in his day-to-day movements.

Consequences of Habitat Fragmentation

As early as 1855, the French ecologist de Candolle observed, "The breakup of a large landmass into smaller units would necessarily lead to the extinction or local extermination of one or more species and the differential preservation of others." One hundred years ago, Bauer described the differences between biological communities of islands that occur near continents and those that are more distant and isolated. He observed that "the flora and fauna of the first group will be more or less harmonic . . . the flora and fauna of the second group will be disharmonic—that is to say, it will be composed of a mixture of forms which have been introduced accidentally from other places" (Bauer 1891).

Fragmenting landscapes into disjunct patches and restricting and isolating wildlife populations by amplifying the risks associated with movement have drastic consequences for the preservation of biological diversity. Biological diversity consists of the combinations of biological matter at many levels of scale, ranging from heritable traits that occur within species to the aesthetics of landscape configurations that attract millions of tourist dollars and support numerous regional economies.

While some would argue we can always maintain genetic diversity in gene banks and species diversity in botanical gardens, zoos, or zoological parks, these approaches can never conserve the unique combinations that occur in nature and are maintained through the constant interplay of ecological forces. In the final analysis, it is the naturally occurring combinations of biological structure that conservationists are concerned with preserving, not simply the genes or the species themselves.

The powerful role contributed by specific combinations of biological diversity is easily demonstrated. For example, the heterozygous combination of genes (a dominant and a recessive) that imparts malaria resistance to humans is considered a positive benefit. But when we strip the heterogeneity from the combination and allow the same genes to occur in the homogeneous state (just recessives), the previously adaptive trait considered to be a benefit turns to the deadly combination that causes sickle-cell anaemia.

Inbreeding is one process leading to the expression of such destructive traits, and organisms that occur in small, isolated populations have few alternatives to inbreeding. In addition to the genetic consequences, fragmentation and isolation cause many other changes such as loss of species that only occur in large patches of uninterrupted habitat; endangerment of low-density, wide-ranging species; and invasion of alien species—in short, a methodical disintegration of our historic natural faunal character. America's wildlife is coming to resemble the disharmonic collection of opportunistic species referred to by Bauer a century ago.

Moreover, most of the tangible products and services derived from wildlife—such as abundant game harvests, protection from waves afforded by corals, or crop pollination—depend upon large and productive populations. Simply saving a species from extinction does not suffice to meet these needs. Preserving only a few remnant individuals or, more simply, their genetic diversity fails to address the larger problem of conserving biological diversity.

The critical stage in the transformation from harmonic wildlife communities to unstructured collections of species is habitat fragmentation. As formerly expansive and contiguous habitats are opened up, fragmented, and isolated, the landscape becomes a haven for human-adapted species and increasingly inhospitable to natural wildlife communities. Wilderness species are held hostage in habitat patches isolated by intensive human alterations of the landscapes such as agricultural and urban/suburban development. [4]

But other forces are also at work. The intrusion of roads, especially multilane interstates and primary highways carrying heavy loads of high-speed traffic, generally has devastating impacts on resident wildlife. When combined, these factors mean that the small mammals, snakes, turtles, salamanders, and frogs inhabiting two tracts of forest divided by a heavily traveled highway may be as effectively isolated from one another as are two populations separated by ten miles of range or forest. In the long run, these habitat fragmenting forces may be more degrading to North America's wildlife populations than actual loss of habitat acreage. [5]

Consider this triple jeopardy: At the same time that development reduces the total amount of habitat, squeezing remaining wildlife into smaller and more isolated patches, the high-speed traffic of larger and wider highways eliminates more and more of the remaining populations.

Habitat fragmentation results in four major consequences for wildlife. First is the loss of deep-woods or area-sensitive species—animals whose occurrence and successful reproduction are highly dependent on the size of the habitat patch in which they occur. For example, numerous species of breeding birds simply do not breed in small patches of forest. [6]

Second, the larger species that normally move widely and occur at low densities under the best of conditions are quickly lost. For example, Florida panthers normally occur at densities of less than one individual per 50,000 acres, a situation caused, in part, by the long distances traveled by individual territorial cats. As they move over great areas, these animals become exposed to more of the dangers associated with humanized environments. Encounters with illegal hunting, traps, high-speed traffic, pets, and livestock predispose the animal to a shorter life span. It is partly because of these wide movements that panthers were considered nuisance animals in former times. All the larger carnivores—badger, fisher, wolf, cougar, bobcat, and bear—have either been eliminated or dramatically reduced and restricted throughout the eastern United States. [7]

Third, when coupled with the loss of native large carnivores, fragmented and human-subsidized landscapes (providing artificial sources of food and shelter) become dominated by alien or already common species. Generally, these species have adapted over thousands of years of close interaction with humans; therefore, they succeed in human-dominated environments. It is no mystery why European species such as pigeons, sparrows, starlings, rats, mice, and carp become such pests in our humanized environment. Similarly, increased populations of raccoons, skunks, opossums, armadillos, and free-ranging dogs and cats depredate the nests of ground-nesting birds, small mammals, turtles, and salamanders, including those of threatened and endangered species such as marine turtles. [8]

Most of these alien and common species survive because of their aggressiveness and tolerance of humans, causing additional problems for the rarer species. European starlings, English sparrows, and red-bellied woodpeckers all compete with less aggressive cavity-nesting birds such as the blue-bird. The brown-headed cowbird, a species that must lay its eggs in the nests of songbirds, was once excluded from the closed forests of the East. But as development opens up more and more forestland, the cowbird, which prefers fragmented and open landscapes, is expanding its range throughout the East and greatly increasing in abundance, parasitizing the nests of forest-dwelling songbirds that occur anywhere within 100 yards of openings.[9] Cowbird nest parasitism is a principal cause of the endangerment of Kirtland's warbler, and it probably was a factor in the recent extinction of Bachman's warbler.

Fourth, inbreeding depression is a logical conse-quence of low densities and isolated populations. Animal geneticists teach that in order to maintain genetic integrity within a strain, several hundred breeding animals are required. Biologists, in turn, witness the effects of inbreeding as lower levels of libido, fertility, and rates of successful reproduc-tion. In studies where inbreeding has been meas-ured, there is a direct relation between the degree of inbreeding and the weight of offspring and lev-els of infant mortality. Even the weight and com-petitive advantage of those animals that survive to the weaning stage is diminished. So, regardless of whether a species is kept alive within the bounds of parks or refuges, there is no assurance that pop-ulations will remain viable over the long term.[10]

Refinements to Successful Conservation Programs

The present body of conservation laws, treaties, and policies; the combined efforts of state, federal, and nongovernmental organizations; and the in-creasing number of state and national parks, forests, and refuges have accomplished spectacular results. Not only are the populations of hundreds of species of wildlife improved over what they were a century ago, the sensitivity and concern of U.S. citi-zens about the role and importance of wildlife have never been as great as now. Conserving renewable resources such as water, wildlife, and wood is important policy by anyone's measure.

The extent of national parks, forests, wildlife refuges, and related state and federal rangelands and military bases now approximates one billion acres. Yet, our labyrinth of conservation structures and activities is not sufficiently integrated or fine-tuned to save America's wildlife during the next century. In every region of the country, wide-rang-ing species already suffer the direct consequences of habitat fragmentation. Because large carnivores tend to range over wide distances and encounter conflict whenever they occur close to humans, even the biggest of our parks and refuges outside Alaska are but small habitat islands to them.[11]

To be sure, many of these problems either did not occur, could not be recognized, or were of lower priority during the first hundred years of our conservation history. Now, decades of land development around our conservation areas and the isolation of remnant populations by gigantic systems of roadways, powerlines, pipelines, and strip developments are increasingly the problems with which we must deal. Until recently, neither the prospects nor the implications of reserves be-coming habitat islands in a human-dominated, high-speed landscape were adequately recognized. We are remiss in further delaying modifications to conservation programs and policies.

Fragmentation and isolation of habitats are criti-cal problems that can be largely alleviated through a series of greenbelts, habitat linkages, wildlife cor-ridors, and riparian buffer strips connecting key parks, refuges, and habitat islands.[12] Recognition of the problem coupled with a commitment to solution thrusts a few states—for example, Florida and Massachussetts—to the forefront of a new era in wildlife conservation. This commitment to solu-tion has been stimulated in rapid-growth areas such as California and the Sunbelt South by the simultaneous phenomena of unrestrained human population growth, unabated increases in traffic and vehicle speeds over ever-expanding multilane highway systems, and increasing knowledge of the movement patterns of large wild animals.

A Strategic Connection

When President Theodore Roosevelt designated Pelican Island along Florida's eastern coast as the nation's first official wildlife refuge, he could not have imagined what would eventually happen around it. He knew that southern Florida's wad-ing bird populations had been plundered during the late 1880s, but he could not have known that the populations would be only one percent as great

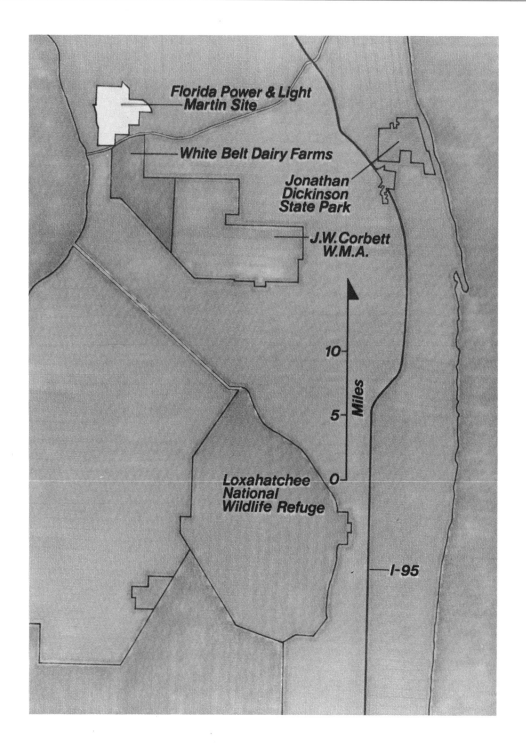

Figure 3. Protected Conservation Areas in Southeastern Florida.

Loxahatchee National Wildlife Refuge is separated from the J.W. Corbett Wildlife Management Area complex by only five miles of private land.

in the 1980s.

Also in southeastern Florida, the Loxahatchee National Wildlife Refuge is the second largest-wildlife refuge in the eastern United States. However, urban sprawl to the east, intensive agricultural use to the west, and rapidly encroaching development pressures to the north dictate that this area will soon be only a small island of natural habitat in a sea of disturbance. The 150,000 acres contained within its bounds can barely support a single Florida panther, much less a viable population.

Just to the north is the 58,000-acre J.W. Corbett Wildlife Management Area, bordered by a 22,000-acre state-owned conservation area, the White Belt Ranch. These extremely costly public investments are also too small to maintain, let alone contain, viable populations of black bear, Everglades mink, red wolf, or Florida panther. [13] The tragedy and the opportunity are that the Corbett complex is separated from the Loxahatchee and 2.5 million acres of contiguous southern Florida conservation lands by only five miles of private land (see figure 3). Adding a small parcel of perhaps 15,000 acres would link all these areas and make them suitable for Florida's remaining native large mammal species—an infinitesimal investment compared to the highly beneficial role these areas can play in "buffering" Everglades National Park from encroaching human populations to the north and east and rising sea levels from the south and west.

Four hundred miles north of the Corbett area is the 160,000-acre Osceola National Forest. Fifteen miles yet farther north (primarily in Georgia) lies the Okefenokee, the largest wildlife refuge in the eastern United States. Since time immemorial, this regional wilderness has functioned as an integrated swampland ecosystem. In 1989, the two areas will finally be legally connected. A bold policy decision by former U.S. Senator Lawton Chiles of Florida added $7 million to the Forest Service appropriation in order to buy America's first strategic landscape linkage connecting two critical federal properties located in two different states and administered by two different federal departments (Interior and Agriculture). Figure 4 is an artist's rendition of this strategic linkage. The combined area, totaling nearly a million acres, provides the potential for reintroduction of captive-bred Florida panthers, whooping cranes, and red

"Among our many efforts to coexist with animals, the idea of establishing inter-connected habitats for wildlife is the most exciting and promising that I know of."

Marjorie Carr, Florida Defenders of the Environment

wolves as well as sufficiently large space to maintain viable populations of numerous other endangered species, including the red-cockaded woodpecker. [14]

Legs, Wings, Flippers, and Fins

Since the time of Aristotle, humans have marveled at the movement of animals, but never before have we been more sensitive to the *need* for animals to move. Both individuals and entire populations move to escape the consequences of winter, to alleviate competition with their parents, and to disperse across the landscape. Like sea turtles, they may move thousands of miles to find the single nesting beach that they were born on 50 years earlier. They move to colonize new areas and to spread their genes into distant populations. They move for food, they move for cover, they move for mates, and they move for refuge from humans. The overwhelming majority of animals must move during some stage of the life cycle.

Salamanders, salmon, sturgeon, and striped bass move between freshwater environments, necessary for their egg and larval life stages, to terrestrial or saltwater environments that suffice for the adults. Alligators and turtles, on the other hand, must migrate onto land to lay their eggs, but the newborn move back to water for their livelihood.

Like animals, plants also need to move, mostly during the reproductive stages. Primitive plants depend on the wind to carry pollen from one individual to another. But wind and water proved too capricious for higher plants, and showy flowers evolved in order to attract beetles, bees, bats, and birds to cross-pollinate the plants. Literally hundreds of economically important plants such as raspberries, blueberries, and strawberries; trees such as apples, oranges, and maples; and crops such as clover, carrots, and cotton depend on animal movement for pollination.[15] Honeybees were introduced into America specifically to move pollen from one crop plant to another. And carry pollen they do. A single bee may visit more than 1,000 flowers to collect a load of pollen, and the average worker carries 10 to 15 loads per day (Winston 1987). Thus, as many as 10,000 flowers may be cross-pollinated by a single bee in a single day. Cross-pollination is roughly synonymous with outbreeding and is the opposite of inbreeding.

Unlike the honeybee that makes thousands of individual, short trips, animals such as panthers, black bears, elk, and caribou travel long distances. Although the average home-range size of all Florida panthers is only 150 square miles, a single dominant male may distribute his genes among individuals covering an area three times as large. He may need to walk as far as 20 miles in a single night. Even river otters may travel five miles a night.[16]

Numerous species that we take for granted simply will not occur in expansive conifer forests or agricultural and urban landscapes when their movement is impeded. Several studies demonstrate that gray squirrels will not occur in fragmented landscapes unless "stringers" (hardwood streamside corridors) allow for dispersal and foraging in otherwise inhospitable landscapes.[17] Turkey managers refer to these stringers as "turkey trots" because they allow turkeys to skulk across open areas that would otherwise constitute barriers to movement.[18] Canadian researchers report, "The most fundamental barrier affecting woodland species in farmland is the separation of forest fragments from each other by creation of crop fields between them. The resulting 'isolation effect' can range from almost complete removal of a species' habitat to limited barriers easily overcome . . . by movement corridors" (Henderson et al. 1985).

Riparian Woods and Rheotaxis

One great principle of physics, gravity, is captured in the observation that "water runs downhill." A similar concept from biology is that of tropism and taxis. Organisms orient and move according to directional stimuli: Plants grow toward light (phototaxis), moths are attracted by smell (chemotaxis), and fish migrate against the current (rheotaxis). Thus, while rivers and streams drain the landscape from higher to lower elevations, many aquatic organisms move themselves, matter, and energy upstream—against the gradient. Sturgeon, salmon, and sea bass move from the sea up rivers to spawn and, in so doing, link the sea to freshwater systems in a "counter-current" or "upstream" direction. Through the processes of ingesting, digesting, and transforming plants and animals, carnivores move energy and matter up the trophic ladder. By foraging at low elevations and moving to higher elevations, animals move materials and energy against the gravitational field. Physicists define this as "work."

An example is found in the thousands of tons of nutrients per annum that are gleaned from estuaries, rivers, lakes, and streams and moved back upslope by colonial water birds through ingestion and defecation. Otters and other furbearers do this work as well. Twenty-six of North America's 30 most common furbearers are either carnivores by diet or are classified as "carnivora" even though they forage more generally—for example, the black bear. The majority of these species are amphibious inasmuch as they are terrestrial mammals that live in close association with aquatic habitats. Animals such as mink and otter forage from the aquatic food chain but spend most of their time in terrestrial habitats. Similar to fish, they do work by moving energy and matter up the gradient against the gravitational field; they link aquatic systems to adjacent uplands.

Carnivores play other roles in the environment as well. Because of their predatory nature, the relatively low density of prey in the environment, and their large home ranges, predators normally utilize numerous habitat types. In this "inverse pyramid" of habitats, animals high in the food chain (such as top carnivores) utilize and integrate food sources from more habitats than animals lower in the food

Figure 4. Protective Designation of Pinhook Swamp Creates a Strategic Linkage Between Osceola National Forest and Okefenokee National Wildlife Refuge.

Drawing by Merald R. Clark

chain (such as herbivores). The number of habitats that an animal ranges over and thus integrates is inverse to its level in the food chain and its abundance. The work wide-ranging animals perform by influencing the relative abundance and distribution of prey animals is generally overlooked by conservation agencies and organizations that define communities on the basis of a couple of dominant plant species. It stands to reason that decision-makers who do not appreciate the role mammalian carnivores play would not design a preserve system to protect them. (Figure 5 shows how animal population growth in Florida is now tending to be inversely related to size and trophic level.)

Rather than presuming the lower trophic levels do not need the higher ones, we must give greater attention to conserving entire faunal and floral assemblages that can function as a natural system. Because flowing water and other gravitational mechanisms move energy and matter toward the lower elevations and because so many animals are amphibious, the junction between land and water is by far the richest of our wildlife habitats. Numerous species of fish, amphibians, reptiles, mammals, and birds not only live there, they also use these riparian or streamside woods as landscape thoroughfares. Thus, even if rivers and riparian woods had no fisheries value, no recreation value, and no hydro-period regulation, water recharge, or cleansing value, we would still choose them as priority wildlife conservation areas. Even if humans were not involved at all, rivers, streams, and drainageways would still portray nature's own energy signature to be read as a resource management template. On the other hand, it is because these stream and riverfront woods have such diverse and strong interest groups that they should be our most quickly designated conservation corridors. Foresters, fisheries managers, recreationists, and water quality managers should all rally to the common goal.

Even though riparian woods represent our single best hope for creating a system of interconnecting corridors, they do not exhaust the opportunity list. Numerous cultural artifacts also meet the design criteria. Abandoned railroad rights-of-way and powerline, pipeline, and other easements can be utilized by mammals. Canopy roads, wooded median strips of interstate highways, windbreaks, greenbelts, and wooded visual screens can be used as corridors by birds. Equestrian trails, jogging trails, and bicycle routes can be of value in urban areas, just as wooded fencerows play a role in rural landscapes. All represent linear connectors that permeate the landscape; all can play a role in an interconnected habitat island system.

We do not necessarily need to purchase these acreages in order to put them to use. In many cases, a form of conservation easement and negotiated land use that facilitates animal passage is all that is needed. We must direct a major effort toward development of incentives and rewards for private landowners who wish to contribute to conservation while keeping their land productive (Harris 1985).

Piecemeal Management for Movement

Scientific journals, agency policy manuals, and conservation law books are filled with examples and mandates for managing animal movement. Most early federal wildlife legislation dealt with protecting the migration habits of, and opportunities for, migrant species. As early as 1914, the federal government entered into an international treaty to protect the movement of migrant birds, and as late as 1987, the United States signed a treaty with Mexico to protect the international migration of monarch butterflys. [19]

Fisheries, waterfowl, and other migrant game management strategies have hinged on the need for birds and fish to migrate. The huge pipeline constructed to carry oil south from Alaska's northern slope was elevated specifically to allow movement of caribou and other tundra game animals. Interstate highway underpasses allow deer and elk to migrate in several western states, and an underpass system in Glacier National Park was designed to improve mountain goat access to mineral licks. Prior to underpass construction, goats were successful in crossing U.S. Route 2 only 74 percent of the time. Research after underpass construction revealed that 100 percent of crossing attempts were eventually successful. [20]

There are also numerous occasions where boundary configurations of parks, preserves, and refuges have been planned to accommodate wildlife movement. Olympic National Park was

Figure 5. Population Growth or Decline as Related to Body Size and Trophic Level for Selected Florida Mammals.

The solid silhouettes depict species, mostly mid-sized and omnivorous, that are increasing in numbers (gray and red fox, raccoon, coyote, opossum, skunk, and armadillo). The species depicted in outline, which tend to be larger or more specifically carnivorous, are declining in numbers or their status is in question (black bear, Florida panther, bobcat, otter, mink, and weasel). The red wolf is already extinct in the wild.

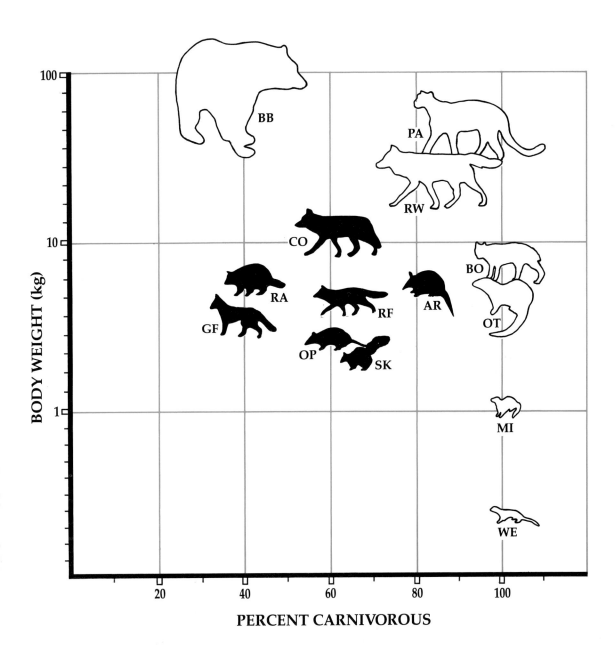

designed to include a 50-mile river valley corridor linking the predominantly high elevation park to the Pacific Ocean shore. When President Harry Truman dedicated the park in 1953, he observed, "Olympic National Park . . . now becomes the only park in the world to extend from snow-capped mountains to ocean beaches." The purpose of the vertical valley corridor is to facilitate migration of deer, salmon, steelhead and other species. [21] In New Jersey, Pinelands National Reserve depends on "corridors near the boundaries of the pinelands and around major towns to delimit and reinforce the integrity of the entire pinelands as a unit. Corridors linking the southern and northern centers of the Pinelands also reinforce the integrity of the whole pinelands and are a special issue for species at the northern or southern edges of their ranges" (Good 1982).

In Costa Rica, a 15-mile-long, 2-mile-wide riverine corridor connects the lowland La Selva Biological Station with the montane Braulio Carrillo National Park (see figure 6). This creates an uninterrupted biological preserve rising from an elevation of 114 feet above sea level to more than 9,500 feet (Pringle et al. 1984). The same prescription was implemented in Tanzania so that elephants could migrate between Lake Manyara National Park and the Ngorongoro Conservation Area. International development agencies (e.g., USAID) required that landscape linkages be built into the Maheweli Ganga hydroelectric project in Sri Lanka so that elephants can continue to utilize traditional migration routes between reserves.

Following the recommendations of renowned conservationist George B. Schaller, the Chinese government "is considering an addition to Wolong as well as the creation of one large reserve in the Min Mountains by conecting the Tangjiahe, Baishuaijiang, Walang and Jiuzhaigou reserves. Where expansion is not feasible, the preservation or reestablishment of corridors of habitat can in some instances prevent neighboring but noncontiguous populations from becoming isolated" (Schaller et al. 1985).

It is clear from these examples that protecting migrant species and their freedom to move and designating landscape corridors to facilitate animal movement are established conservation practices in this country and abroad. However, our efforts

to date have been isolated instances directed at individual species or problems. With the exception of migratory bird management, there has been no overriding or unified philosophy to direct state or regional conservation planning.

Allowing Entire Faunas To Move

Thirty-eight years before the Declaration of Independence, approximately one hundred black slaves escaped from British plantations and established Fort Mose in Spanish Florida. This was the first free black settlement in North America. Several 18th century maps made by Spanish engineers show the fort in the center of high farmland, where the residents grew corn and millet. Today, however, the site of Mose occurs in a submerged marsh near the edge of the Atlantic, victim of the rising sea. [22]

When Theodore Roosevelt and other conservation leaders of the early 20th century spent holidays at the coast, Cape May, New Jersey was one of eastern North America's most famous resort beaches. Today, the beach is nearly gone, the city has dwindled, and the narrow strip of land that was formerly coastal plain has become part of the continental shelf, victim of the encroaching sea. Everglades National Park in southern Florida was America's first national park established to preserve wildlife and natural ecosystem diversity. It is also one of the first national parks to be jeopardized by rising sea levels and the advancing shore. Southern Florida's flat landscape means a one-foot rise in sea level causes a 10-mile northward migration of Florida Bay. [23] Climatologists now predict that, as a result of the greenhouse effect, the next one-foot rise in sea level may occur as early as the year 2015 (e.g., see Hansen et al. 1988). At best, State Road 27—presently taking visitors overland to Everglades National Park headquarters—will become a causeway across Florida Bay.

Thirty-five 100-foot-long aquatic underpasses are presently being constructed beneath the Interstate 75 extension across southern Florida from Naples to Fort Lauderdale. Farsighted decision-makers such as Senator Bob Graham and Governor Bob Martinez of Florida have seen this as an essential step to allow water, fauna, and flora to move beneath the otherwise barricading interstate embankment. In addition to allowing Everglades

Figure 6. A Riparian Corridor in Costa Rica Connecting La Selva Biological Station with Braulio Carrillo National Park.

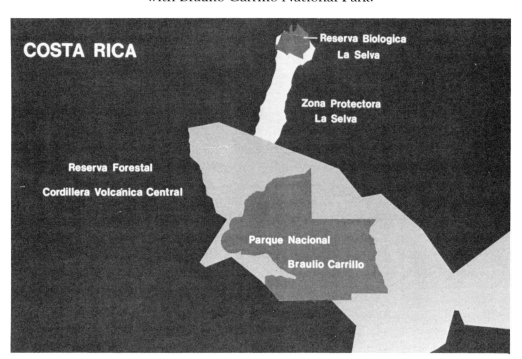

mink and otter to move with their fisheries prey base, the underpasses will permit black bears and panthers to avoid the perils of ever-increasing automobile traffic loads and thousands of fresh-water and estuarine species to migrate northward as the salt of Florida Bay crystallizes on remnant rootstocks of former forests. Without the under-passes, the I-75 extension would prevent these species from moving northward with the pull of receding glaciers and the push of a rising sea.

Accelerated rates of climate change and rising sea levels require implementation of conservation strategies to allow for the displacement of entire communities of plants and animals from their pre-sent locations. While north-south migration corri-dors will be necessary in most cases, mountainous areas and areas near the sea will require corridors that span elevational gradients. Natural landscape features such as floodplains, river valleys, and ridge tops have guided the movement of plant and animal associations for millenia and should now serve as our design templates for an integrated sys-tem of ecological preserves for the future. [24]

The Next Steps

A new strategy is called for, one that transcends piecemeal land consolidation here, more riparian corridors there, and another underpass out yonder. We need to replace the 19th century notion that the job is done when we succeed in designating certain areas as parks, refuges, or national forests. At that point, the task has only begun. We must adopt realistic approaches regarding the need for natural ecosystems to change and interact with their sur-roundings. What happens to the habitat content within a preserve may be less important than what happens in the surrounding contextual setting. Not only do animals need to move back and forth in a dynamic landscape; the preserves themselves may need to move.

As long as we limit our focus to problems with-in park or refuge boundaries, even the largest parks and refuges will not conserve our native fauna: Most will be too small for viable popula-tions. Some will experience natural disasters, and some will become submerged beneath the sea.

Without fanfare and frequently without notice, native faunal integrity will continue to erode. The public may never notice this erosion until the death of the last individual of a species claims all the attention; meanwhile, even the large conservation areas will be experiencing faunal collapse.

We may not need more public domain acres; but we most assuredly will need different acres and different configurations. Nearly 40 percent of the land area of the United States is already in public ownership, managed by state and federal agencies. We need to reevaluate conservation policies on this land, most of which is not administered to conserve biological diversity. Air Force bases and National Guard reservations may be just as critical to plant and animal movement as are national parks, forests, and wildlife refuges.

We may not need more programs; but we do need better program integration and agency cooperation. To date, our initiatives have been stacking up, but they have not been adding up. A modest increase in the federal excise tax on gasoline would help the balance of trade and the U.S. economy, reduce the burning of carbon fuels, and slow the greenhouse effect. It could help finance the construction and retrofitting of underpasses in federal highway systems, working for the conservation of America's biological resources rather than against them.

We need more than big linkages between big areas for big mammals; we also need citizens and administrators who understand the need for movement at all scales. Fencerows connecting woodlots and abandoned acres are just as important to midwestern wildlife as streamside buffers are to western mountain species. Greenways accommodating linear outdoor recreation such as jogging, bicycling, horseback riding, canoeing, and cross-country skiing can be as useful for wildlife as they are for people.

We need not just analysis, but application; not just policies, but practical programs; not just individual actions, but integrated action. We do not need to set the United States aside as a tribute to the past; we need to develop new linkages that will function in the future.

Larry D. Harris has taught and conducted research since 1972 at the University of Florida, specializing in forest management for biological diversity. He earned his M.S. and Ph.D. degrees in ecology and systems ecology from Michigan State University, with postdoctoral work in systems ecology through the U.S. International Biological Program. He is the author of more than 50 scientific publications and sits on several policy and research review boards on maintaining biodiversity. Dr. Harris's book The Fragmented Forest, *published in 1984, won national and international awards for excellence.*

Peter B. Gallagher has served as a staff writer for the St. Petersburg Times and is now engaged in free-lance writing assignments on environmental issues, particularly those affecting southern Florida. He is president of Save the Panther, Inc., in Tampa, Florida.

Footnotes

[1] Technical details of the bear's movement are given in Maehr et al. 1988. An exemplary summary of black bear dispersal characteristics is given in Rogers 1987. The most recent compilations of relevant black bear information for the eastern United States are Maehr and Brady 1984 and Carlock et al. 1983. Wooding and Brady 1986 report Florida black bear roadkill statistics.

[2] Critics of the dispersal corridor approach commonly argue that even if we commit to preserving corridor habitats we would have no assurance that animals would use them. This criticism is ill-founded. Thousands of species migrate seasonally but not in random directions. For example, when roadkill statistics are plotted on maps, it is possible to discern "hot spots" where most of the fatalities occur. Chanin and Jefferies 1978 observe, "Mortality records collected by one of us (PRFC) show that in some areas, otters have repeatedly been found dead on the roads at the same spot over a number of years . . . ." This same pattern holds for black bear and other species in Florida.

[3] Lalo 1987 presents a recent account of roadkill mortality on America's highways and puts the annual toll at 100 million animals per year. Oxley et al. 1974, Leedy 1975, Leedy et al. 1975, Adams and Geis 1981, and Mader 1984 should be consulted for entry into the literature on wildlife and highways. See O'Shea 1988 for manatee information and U.S. Fish and Wildlife Service 1987 and Belden 1988 regarding the Florida panther.

[4] Wilcox and Murphy 1985 state that "habitat fragmentation is the most serious threat to biological diversity and is the primary cause of the present extinction crisis." Major regional analyses of the problem are presented by Burgess and Sharpe 1981, Harris 1984, and Saunders et al. 1987. Additional key papers that address individual groups of animals or specific situations are Robbins 1979, Howe 1984, Lynch and Whigham 1984, Wilcove et al. 1986, Wilcove 1987, and Harris 1989.

[5] The full body of knowledge regarding the effects of habitat fragmentation and the importance of corridors derives from many different approaches. Critics commonly deny the consequences of habitat fragmentation and imply that linkages or interconnecting corridors are somehow artificial management contraptions. It is, in fact, the fragmented landscape that represents the artificial from the point of view of native fauna. Arguments that the theory of island biogeography has not been "proven" are equally erroneous inasmuch as abundant empirical support for the value of habitat corridors derives from many sources, some predating MacArthur and Wilson's work by half a century.

Entry into traditional biogeography literature is provided by Darlington 1957. Primary theoretical issues are reviewed by Preston 1962, MacArthur and Wilson 1967, Simberloff 1974, Brown and Kodric-Brown 1977, and Margules et al. 1982. The combination of logic and observation leading to recommendations is put forth by Diamond 1975, Terborgh 1974, Wilson and Willis 1975, and Wilcox 1980, among others.

Entry into the extensive research and management literature can be pursued as follows: The oldest body of support and that which deals with the largest scale of time and space is paleontology. George G. Simpson (e.g., 1940; 1965) is perhaps most effective at articulating the importance of land bridges as dispersal corridors for terrestrial organisms. Both the continental (e.g., Adams 1902; Webb and Wilkins 1984) and the island (e.g., Darlington 1957) divisions of biogeography literature attest to the importance of direct linkages as dispersal avenues. Patterson 1984 and Heany and Patterson 1986 provide entry into the literature on regional patterns of mammal distribution as affected by dispersal corridors.

The importance of linear, interconnecting habitats such as fencerows, field borders, and roadside verges for wildlife in agricultural landscapes has been known for more than 50 years. A large body of literature dealing with many small game species exists (e.g., Grange and McAtee 1934; Sumner 1936; Lehmann 1937; Edminster 1938; Davison 1939 and 1941; Dambach 1942, 1945, and 1948; Graham 1944 and 1947; Petrides 1942).

One group of animals that has been particularly well studied and one for which virtually all authorities advocate the use of wooded corridors is the squirrels. For example, it was known nearly 50 years ago (see Baumgartner 1943, Allen 1943, and Flyger and Gates 1982) that squirrel populations of small and widely separated woodlots are sometimes "shot out" and restocking does not occur by dispersing squirrels unless travel lanes such as wooded fencerows are available.

There is a large literature associated with the wildlife corridor value of linear strips of forest such as streamside buffers, riparian forests, and shelterbelts (e.g., Munns and Stoeckeler 1946; MacClintock et al. 1977; Robbins 1979; Whitcomb et al. 1981; Arnold 1982; Landers 1985; Wilcove et al. 1986; Lynch 1987). Australian forest wildlife ecologists have focused a great deal on this topic. For example, Suckling 1982 observes, "The size of reserves is not relevant, provided they are linked by corridors of suitable habitat, as gene flow and dispersal can occur freely throughout. Within intensively managed forest areas a system of linked reserves is desirable

. . . ." Loyn 1985 observes that "such retained areas provide a valuable system of mature habitats for flora and fauna. Their value can be enhanced by strategic linking of reserves and by deliberate selection of retained areas for value as wildlife habitat."

[6] As early as 1944, Charles Kendeigh distinguished between species that were characteristic of different forest types and those that were more opportunistic. He referred to the former as interior species and the latter as exterior species. More recently, authorities such as Chandler Robbins (e.g., 1979) have used the phrase "area-sensitive" to describe those species requiring substantial tracts of forest to survive. Technically, there is a distinction between interior species that require extensive tracts of closed-canopy forest and area-sensitive species that require large areas but may be more tolerant of forest management operations. Papers by Wilcove constitute up-to-date reviews of current scientific literature. Data-based papers specific to the Southeast are Harris and Wallace 1984, Cox 1988, and Harris 1989.

[7] Matthiae and Stearns 1981 describe the effects of forest fragmentation and its consequences on the large mammals of the north central states. Harris et al. 1982 describe the differential loss of the wide-ranging carnivores from the fragmented habitats of the Cascade Mountains. Maehr 1984 illustrates and Pelton 1986 describes how the loss of movement corridors has come to isolate and restrict the distribution of black bears to large tracts of federal lands in the eastern United States.

[8] The effects of raccoon predation on the nests of marine turtles, gopher tortoises, alligators, and game birds have been known for a considerable time. More recently, the effects of amplified levels of middle-sized omnivores as ground nest depredators have been identified as a critical factor in the demise of several species of migrant songbirds. This process of middle-sized omnivore amplification is sometimes referred to as "meso-mammal release" (see Soule et al. 1988, Harris 1988c, and Harris 1989).

[9] Stanley Temple and associates at the University of Wisconsin have published most extensively on the cowbird problem (e.g., Ambuel and Temple 1983; Brittingham and Temple 1984) as it relates to edge-effects management. Harris 1988d provides an overview of the issues that surround game management techniques such as patch cuts designed to create edge effects. Three additional papers in the same issue of *Conservation Biology* (Vol. 2, No. 4) portray the scope of the edge-effect controversy.

[10] Some of the best research results and summaries are published by Ralls and associates (e.g., 1986; 1988). Dr. Melody Roelke is conducting research on the effects of inbreeding in Florida panthers (see U.S. Fish and Wildlife Service 1987). The collection of papers in Soule 1987 provides the most recent synthesis of management for viable populations.

[11] Individual national parks, wildlife refuges, and even the larger national forests are simply not large enough in and of themselves to support viable populations of numerous species of wildlife, especially the territorial and wide-ranging mammals. For example, only two or three national wildlife refuges in the eastern United States are large enough to support a single pair of panthers; none could support a viable population. Newmark 1987 describes the essentials of the extinction process in the parks of the western United States. Although his data base and analyses are now being criticized (e.g., Quinn et al. 1989), the underlying premise of his conclusions remains valid. Harris 1984 and Salwasser et al. 1987 describe the necessity of interagency management strategies in order to provide expanses of landscape sufficiently large to maintain viable populations and mitigate the problems of isolated parks.

[12] The various terms applied to linear conservation lands reflect diverse origins of the same general concept. **Greenways** is commonly used in urban and regional planning, and the process of creating greenway networks is referred to as greenlining. An entire school of planning philosophy hinges on naturally occurring environmental corridors (see Belknap et al. 1967, Katz and Sollen 1976, Walesh l976, Davis and Glick 1978, Rubin and Emmerich 1981, Corbett 1983, Poynton and Roberts 1985, and Adams and Dove 1989).

The importance of **linear habitats** such as fencerows and windbreaks was introduced in note 5. Throughout much of Europe, especially in England, the utility of hedgerows as wildlife habitat has been a major concern for decades (see Doudeswell 1987 and Pollard et al. 1979). Highway verges, median strips, and rights-of-way have long been advocated for wildlife habitat (e.g., Latham 1956; Egler 1952, 1957; Smith 1970; Way 1970). Fisheries biologists are strong advocates of streamside buffer strips that protect aquatic habitats, and, more recently, the forestry profession has committed to the use of streamside buffers as a means of managing water quality and hydrology.

The concept of **landscape linkages** to connect existing parks and reserves seems to make more sense to the general public, legislators, and decision-makers who readily grasp the value of consolidating existing but soon-to-be isolated natural areas.

Report prepared by the Landscape Architecture Research Office, Graduate School of Design, Harvard University. The Conservation Foundation, Washington, D.C.

Blackner, L. 1986. Saving pieces of paradise: Wildlife corridors. *Environmental and Land Use Law Section Reporter* 9 (2): 28-32.

Brady, J., and D. Maehr. 1985. Distribution of black bears in Florida. *Florida Field Naturalist* 13 (1): 1-24.

Brittingham, M., and S. Temple. 1983. Have cowbirds caused forest songbirds to decline? *BioScience* 33 (1): 31-35.

Brooker, M. 1983. Conservation of wildlife in river corridors. *Nature in Wales* 2: 11-20.

Brown, J., and A. Kodric-Brown. 1977. Turnover rates in insular biogeography: Effect of immigration on extinction. *Ecology* 58: 445-449.

Brown, M., and J. Schaefer. 1988. Buffer zones for water, wetlands, and wildlife. Center for Wetlands, University of Florida, Tallahassee, Florida.

Burgess, R., and D. Sharp, eds. 1981. Forest island dynamics in man-dominated landscapes. Springer Verlag, New York.

Carlock, D., R. Conley, J. Collins, P. Hale, K. Johnson, A. Johnson, and M. Pelton. 1983. The tri-state black bear study. Technical Report 83-9. Tennessee Wildlife Resources Agency, Knoxville, Tennessee.

Chanin, P., and D. Jefferies. 1978. The decline of otter, *Lutra lutra L.* in Britain: An analysis of hunting records and discussion of causes. *Biological Journal of the Linnean Society* 10: 305-328.

Collins, B., and W. Russell. 1987. Protecting the New Jersey pinelands: A new direction in land-use management. Rutgers University Press, New Brunswick, New Jersey.

Corbett, M. 1983. Greenline parks, land conservation trends for the eighties and beyond. National Parks and Conservation Association, Washington, D.C.

Cox, J. 1988. The influence of forest size on transient and resident bird species occupying maritime hammocks of northeastern Florida. *Florida Field Naturalist* 16 (2): 25-56.

Crawford, M. 1988. Planning for climate change. Article based on draft report on the potential effects of global climate change on the United States. U.S. Environmental Protection Agency. *Science* 242: 510.

Curatolo, J., and S. Murphy. 1988. The effects of pipelines, roads, and traffic on the movements of caribou, *Rangifer tarandus*. *The Canadian Field Naturalist* 100: 218-224.

Dambach, C. 1942. Fence row facts. *Soil Conservation* 7: 238.

_____. 1945. Some biologic and economic aspects of field border management. In *Transactions of the North American Wildlife Conference* 10: 169-184.

_____. 1948. New lessons from old plantings. *Journal of Soil and Water Conservation* 3: 165-190.

Darlington, P., Jr. 1957. Zoogeography: The geographical distribution of animals. John Wiley and Sons, New York.

Davis, A., and T. Glick. 1978. Urban ecosystems and island biogeography. *Environmental Conservation* 5 (4): 299-304.

Davison, V. 1939. Protecting field borders. Leaflet 188. U.S. Department of Agriculture, Washington, D.C.

_____. 1941. Wildlife borders—an innovation in farm management. *Journal of Wildlife Management* 5: 390-394.

de Candolle, A. in Browne, J. 1983. The secular ark, studies in the history of biogeography. Yale University Press, New Haven, Connecticut.

Dendy, T. 1987. Working group on the value of corridors (and design features of same) and small patches of habitat. Chapter 40 in D. Saunders, G. Arnold, A. Burbidge, and A. Hopkins, eds. Nature conservation: The role of remnants of native vegetation. Surrey Beatty and Sons Pty. Limited, Chipping Norton, NSW, Australia.

Diamond, J. 1975. The island dilemma: Lessons of modern biogeographic studies for the design of natural reserves. *Biological Conservation* 7: 129-146.

_____. 1976. Island biogeography and conservation: Strategy and limitations. *Science* 193: 1027-1029.

Dickson, J., and J. Huntley. 1987. Riparian zones and wildlife in southern forests: The problem and squirrel relationships. In J. Dickson and O. Maughan, eds. Managing southern forests for wildlife and fish. General Technical Report SO-65. Forest Service, U.S. Department of Agriculture, Washington, D.C.

Doudeswell, W. 1987. Hedgerows and verges. Allen and Unwin, Boston.

Edminster, F. 1938. The farm fence in wildlife management and erosion control. In *Transactions of the North American Wildlife Conference* 3: 583-591.

Egler, F. 1952. Transmission lines as wildlife habitat. *The Land* 11: 149-152.

_____. 1957. Rights-of-way and wildlife habitat: A progress report. In *Transactions of the North American Wildlife Conference* 22: 133-144.

Eide, S., S. Miller, and M. Chihuly. 1988. Oil pipeline crossing sites utilized in winter by moose, *Alces alces,* and caribou, *Rangifer tarandus,* in southcentral Alaska. *The Canadian Field Naturalist* 100: 197-207.

Fahrig, L., L. Lefkovitch, and G. Merriam. 1983. Population stability in a patchy environment. In W. Lauenroth, G. Skogerboe, and M. Flug, eds. Analysis of ecological systems: State-of-the-art in ecological modelling. Elsevier, New York.

Fahrig, L., and G. Merriam. 1985. Habitat patch connectivity and population survival. *Ecology* 66: 1762-1768.

Fenner, F., ed. 1975. A national system of ecological reserves in Australia. Report No. 19. Australian Academy of Science, Canberra, Australia.

Flyger, V., and J. Gates. 1982. Fox and gray squirrels. In J. Chapman and G. Feldhamer, eds. Wild mammals of North America. Johns Hopkins University Press, Baltimore, Maryland.

Forman, R. 1981. Interaction among landscape elements: A core of landscape ecology. In *Proceedings of the International Congress, Society of Landscape Ecology.* Wageningen, The Netherlands.

_____. 1983. Corridors in a landscape: Their ecological structure and function. *Ekologiya* (CSSR) 2: 375-387.

_____. 1987. The ethics of isolation, the spread of disturbance, and landscape ecology. In M. Turner, ed. Landscape heterogeneity and disturbance. Springer Verlag, New York.

Forman, R., and J. Baudry. 1984. Hedgerows and hedgerow networks in landscape ecology. *Environmental Management* 8: 495-510.

Forman, R., and M. Godron. 1986. Landscape ecology. John Wiley and Sons, New York.

Gehrken, G. 1975. Travel corridor technique of wild turkey management. In L. Halls, ed. *Proceedings of the Third National Wild Turkey Symposium.* Texas Chapter of the Wildlife Society, Austin, Texas.

Good, R. 1982. Ecological solutions to environmental management concerns in the Pinelands National Reserve. Conference proceedings. Center for Coastal and Environmental Studies, The State University of New Jersey, New Brunswick, New Jersey.

Graham, E. 1944. Natural principles of land use. Oxford University Press, New York.

_____. 1947. The land and wildlife. Oxford University Press, New York.

Grange, W., and W. McAtee. 1934. Improving the farm environment for wildlife. Farmers Bulletin No. 1719. U.S. Department of Agriculture, Washington, D.C.

Green, B. 1985. Countryside conservation. 2nd ed. Allen and Unwin, Boston.

Hansen, J., I. Fung, A. Lacis, S. Lebedeff, D. Rind, R. Ruedy, G. Russell, and P. Stone. 1988. Prediction of near-term climate evolution: What can we tell decision-makers now? In *Preparing for Climate Change: Proceedings of the First North American Conference on Preparing for Climate Change.* Climate Institute, Rockville, Maryland.

Harestad, A., and F. Bunnell. 1979. Home range and body weight—a re-evaluation. *Ecology* 60: 389-402.

Harris, L. 1983. An island archipelago model for maintaining biotic diversity in old-growth forests. In *New forests for a changing world: Proceedings of the Society of American Foresters National Convention.* Society of American Foresters, Portland, Oregon.

_____. 1984. The fragmented forest: Island biogeography theory and the preservation of biotic diversity. University of Chicago Press, Chicago.

_____. 1985. Conservation corridors, a highway system for wildlife. ENFO report 85-5. Florida Conservation Foundation, Winter Park, Florida.

_____. 1988a. Landscape linkages: The dispersal corridor approach to wildlife conservation. *Transactions of the North American Wildlife and Natural Resources Conference* 53: 595-607.

_____. 1988b. Landscape linkages: The dispersal corridor approach to wildlife conservation. VCR film. Florida Films Inc., Gainesville, Florida.

_____. 1988c. The nature of cumulative impacts on the biotic diversity of wetland vertebrates. *Environmental Management* 12 (5): 675-693.

_____. 1988d. Edge effects and conservation of biotic diversity. *Conservation Biology* 2 (4): 330-332.

_____. 1989. The faunal significance of fragmentation of southeastern bottomland forests. In D. Hook, ed. Forested wetlands of the South. Forest Service General Technical Report SE. In press. U.S. Department of Agriculture, Washington, D.C.

Harris, L., and J. Eisenberg. 1988. Enhanced linkages: Necessary steps for success in conservation of faunal diversity. Chapter 17 in M. Pearl and D. Western, eds. Conservation for the 21st century. In press. Oxford University Press, Oxford, England.

Harris, L., and P. Kangas. 1988. Reconsideration of the habitat concept. *Transactions of the North American Wildlife and Natural Resources Conference* 53: 137-144.

Harris, L., C. Maser, and A. Mckee. 1982. Patterns of old growth harvest and implications for Cascades wildlife. *Transactions of the North American Wildlife and Natural Resources Conference* 47: 374-392.

Harris, L., and R. Wallace. 1984. Breeding bird species in Florida forest fragments. *Proceedings of the Annual Conference of the Southeastern Association of Fish and Wildlife Agencies* 83: 87-96.

Hartzog, G. Jr. 1972. Management considerations for optimum development and protection of national park resources. In N. Elliott, ed. Second World Conference on National Parks. International Union for Conservation of Nature and National Resources, Morges, Switzerland.

Heaney, L., and B. Patterson. 1986. Island biogeography of mammals. *Journal of the Linnean Society* 28 (1 and 2): 1-271.

Hedrick, L. 1973. Silvicultural practices and tree squirrels *(Sciurus l.)* in east Texas. Unpublished (M.S. thesis). Texas A & M University, College Station, Texas.

Henderson, M., G. Merriam, and J. Wegner. 1985. Patchy environments and species survival: Chipmunks in an agricultural mosaic. *Biological Conservation* 31: 95-105.

Howe, R. 1984. Local dynamics of bird assemblages in small forest habitat islands in Australia and North America. *Ecology* 65: 1093-1106.

Hunter, M. Jr., G. Jacobson Jr., and T. Webb III. 1989. Paleoecology and the coarse-filter approach to maintaining biological diversity. In press. *Conservation Biology* 3 (1).

International Union for Conservation of Nature and Natural Resources. 1980. With United Nations Environmental Program, World Wildlife Fund, the United Nations Food and Agriculture Organization, and the United Nations Educational, Scientific and Cultural Organization. World conservation strategy. Gland, Switzerland.

Jackson, J. 1976. "Rights-of-way" management for an endangered species—the red-cockaded woodpecker. In *Proceedings of the First National Symposium on Environmental Concerns in Rights-of-way Management.* Mississippi State University, Starkville, Mississippi.

_____. 1987. The red-cockaded woodpecker. *Audubon Wildlife Report* 3: 479-493.

Jewell, P. 1966. The concept of home range in mammals. *Symposia of the Zoological Society of London* 18: 85-109.

Karr, J., and I. Schlosser. 1978. Water resources and the land-water interface. *Science* 201: 229-234.

Katz, J., and J. Sollen. 1976. A backward glance: Environmental corridors of yesterday and today. *Technical Record Bibliography* 3 (6): 65-79. Southeastern Wisconsin Regional Planning Commission, Waukesha, Wisconsin.

Kendeigh, C. 1944. Measurements of bird populations. *Ecological Monographs* 14: 67-106.

Klein, D. 1980. Reaction of caribou and reindeer to obstructions—a reassessment. In E. Reimers, E. Gaare, and S. Skjenneberg, eds. *Proceedings of the Reindeer/Caribou Symposium* 2: 519-527. Roros, Norway.

Laitin, J. 1987. Corridors for wildlife. *American Forests* (September-October): 47-49.

Lalo, J. 1987. The problem of road kill. *American Forests* (September-October): 50-52, 72.

Landers, J. 1985. Integrating wildlife and timber management in southern pine forests. Forest Management Guidelines No. 8. International Paper Company, Bainbridge, Georgia.

Latham, R. 1956. Rights-of-way for wildlife. *Pennsylvania Game News* 27: 19-23.

Leedy, D. 1975. Highway-wildlife relationships: Volume 1, a state of-the-art-report. Report No. FHWA-RD-76-4. Federal Highway Administration, U.S. Department of Transportation, Washington, D.C.

Leedy, D., T. Franklin, and E. Hekimian. 1975. Highway-wildlife relationships: Volume 2, an annotated bibliography. Report No. FHWA-RD-76-5. Federal Highway Administration, U.S. Department of Transportation, Washington, D.C.

Lehmann, V. 1937. Increase quail by improving their habitat. Texas Game, Fish, and Oyster Commission, Austin, Texas.

Loyn, R. 1985. Strategies for conserving wildlife in commercially productive eucalypt forest. *Australian Forestry* 48 (2): 95-101.

Lynch, J. 1987. Responses of breeding bird communities to forest fragmentation. In D. Saunders, G. Arnold, A. Burbidge, and A. Hopkins, eds. Nature conservation, the role of remnants of native vegetation. Surrey Beatty and Sons Pty Limited, Chipping Norton, NSW, Australia.

Lynch, J., and D. Whigham. 1984. Effects of forest fragmentation on breeding bird communities in Maryland, USA. *Biological Conservation* 28: 287-324.

MacArthur, R., and E. Wilson. 1967. The theory of island biogeography. Princeton University Press, Princeton, New Jersey.

MacClintock, L., R. Whitcomb, and B. Whitcomb. 1977. Island biogeography and habitat islands of eastern forest, part II: Evidence for the value of corridors and minimization of isolation in preservation of biotic diversity. *American Birds* 31: 6-16.

Mader, H. 1984. Animal habitat isolation by roads and agricultural fields. *Biological Conservation* 29: 81-96.

Maehr, D. 1984. Distribution of black bears in eastern North America. In D. Maehr and J. Brady, eds. *Proceedings of the Seventh Eastern Workshop on Black Bear Research and Management* 7: 74. Florida Game and Freshwater Fish Commission, Gainesville, Florida.

Maehr, D., and J. Brady, eds. 1984. *Proceedings of the Seventh Eastern Workshop on Black Bear Research and Management.* Florida Game and Freshwater Fish Commission, Gainesville, Florida.

Maehr, D., J. Layne, E. Land, J. McCown, and J. Root. 1988. Long distance movements of a Florida black bear. *Florida Field Naturalist* 16 (1): 1-6.

Mapston, R., R. Zobell, K. Winter, and W. Dooley. 1970. A pass for antelope in sheep-tight fences. *Journal of Range Management* 23 (6): 457-459.

Margules, C., A. Higgs, and R. Rafe. 1982. Modern biogeographic theory: Are there any lessons for nature reserve design? *Biological Conservation* 21: 79-109.

Matthiae, P., and F. Stearns. 1981. Mammals in forest islands in southeast Wisconsin. In R. Burgess and D. Sharpe eds. Forest island dynamics in man-dominated landscapes. Springer Verlag, New York.

McElfresh, R., J. Inglis, and B. Brown. 1980. Gray squirrel usage of hardwood ravines within pine plantations. *Proceedings of Annual Louisiana State University Forestry Symposium* 19: 79-89.

Merriam, G. 1984. Connectivity: A fundamental ecological characteristic of landscape pattern. In J. Brandt and P. Agger, eds. Methodology in landscape ecological research and planning. Roskilde, Denmark.

Methow Valley Citizens Council, et al. plaintiffs-appellants, v. Regional Forester, et al. defendants-appellees. 1987. Opinion No. 86-4108 D.C. No. 85-2124-DA. U.S. District Court for the District of Oregon.

Middleton, J. 1980. Roadside vegetation, a habitat for wildlife. In Roadsides of today and tomorrow. Roadsides Conservation Committee, Victoria, British Columbia.

Middleton, J., and G. Merriam. 1983. Distribution of woodland species in farmland woods. *Journal of Applied Ecology* 20: 623-644.

Munns, E., and J. Stoeckeler. 1946. How are the Great Plains shelterbelts? *Journal of Forestry* 44: 237-257.

New Jersey Pinelands Commission. 1980. Draft comprehensive management plan. New Jersey Pinelands Commission, New Lisbon, New Jersey.

Newmark, W. 1987. A land-bridge perspective on mammalian extinctions in western North American parks. *Nature* 325: 430-432.

Newton, R. 1988. Forested wetlands of the northeast. Publication No. 88-1. Environmental Institute, University of Massachusetts, Amherst, Massachusetts.

Nixon, C., M. McClain, and R. Donohoe. 1980. Effects of clear-cutting on gray squirrels. *Journal of Wildlife Management* 44 (2): 403-412.

Noss, R. 1983. A regional landscape approach to maintain diversity. *BioScience* 33: 700-706.

_____. 1987. Corridors in real landscapes: A reply to Simberloff and Cox. *Conservation Biology* 1 (2): 159-164.

_____. 1987. Protecting natural areas in fragmented landscapes. *Natural Areas Journal* 7: 2-13.

Noss, R., and L. Harris. 1986. Nodes, networks, and MUM's: Preserving diversity at all scales. *Environmental Management* 10: 299-309.

Office of Technology Assessment. 1984. Technologies to sustain tropical forest resources. Report OTA-F-214. Office of Technology Assessment, U.S. Congress, Washington D.C.

_____. 1985. Technologies to benefit agriculture and wildlife. Report OTA-BP-F-34. Office of Technology Assessment, U.S. Congress, Washington D.C.

O'Shea, T. 1988. The problems, potentials and future of manatees in the southeastern United States: Realities, misunderstandings and enigmas. In R. Odom, K. Riddleberger, and J. Ozier, eds. *Proceedings of the Third Southeastern Nongame and Endangered Species Symposium.* Georgia Department of Natural Resources, Social Circle, Georgia.

Oxley, D., M. Fenton, and G. Carmody. 1974. The effects of roads on populations of small mammals. *Journal of Applied Ecology* 11: 51-59.

Patterson, B. 1984. Mammalian extinction and biogeography in the southern Rocky Mountains. In M. Nitecki, ed. Extinctions. University of Chicago Press, Chicago.

Pedevillano, C., and R. Wright. 1987. The influence of visitors on mountain goat activities in Glacier National Park, Montana. *Biological Conservation* 39: 1-11.

Pelton, M. 1986. Habitat needs of black bears in the East. In D. Kulhavy and R. Conner, eds. Wilderness and natural areas in the eastern United States: A management challenge. Center for Applied Studies, School of Forestry, Stephen F. Austin State University, Nacogdoches, Texas.

Peters, R., and J. Darling. 1985. The greenhouse effect and nature reserves. *BioScience* 35 (11): 707-717.

Petrides, G. 1942. Relation of hedgerows in winter to wildlife in central New York. *Journal of Wildlife Management* 6 (4): 261-280.

Pilkey, O. Jr., D. Sharma, H. Wanless, L. Doyle, O. Pilkey, W. Neal, and B. Gruver. 1984. Living with the east Florida shore. Duke University Press, Durham, North Carolina.

Pollard, E., M. Hooper, and N. Moore. 1979. Hedges. W. Collins and Sons, London.

Poynton, J., and D. Roberts. 1985. Urban open space planning in South Africa: A biogeographical perspective. *South African Journal of Science* 81: 33-37.

Prescott-Allen, C., and R. Prescott-Allen. 1986. The first resource, wild species in the North American economy. Yale University Press, New Haven, Connecticut.

Preston, F. 1962. The canonical distribution of commonness and rarity. *Ecology* 43: 185-215, 410-432.

President's Commission on Americans Outdoors. 1987. Americans outdoors: The report of the President's Commission. Island Press, Washington, D.C.

Pringle, C., I. Chacon, M. Grayum, H. Greene, G. Hartshorn, G. Schatz, G. Stiles, C. Gomez, and M. Rodriguez. 1984. Natural history observations and ecological evaluation of the La Selva Protection Zone, Costa Rica. *Brenesia* 22: 189-206.

Purdy, B., ed. 1988. Wet site archaeology. Telford Press, Caldwell, New Jersey.

Quinn, J., C. Van Riper III, and H. Salwasser. 1989. Mammalian extinctions from national parks in the western United States. In press. *Ecology*.

Ralls, K., P. Harvey, and A. Lyles. 1986. Inbreeding in natural populations of birds and mammals. In M. Soule, ed. Conservation biology: The science of scarcity and diversity. Sinauer Associates, Sunderland, Massachusetts.

Ralls, K., J. Ballou, and A. Templeton. 1988. Estimates of lethal equivalents and the cost of inbreeding in mammals. *Conservation Biology* 2 (2): 185-193.

Readers Digest Association. 1984. The patchwork landscape: The living countryside. Reader's Digest Association Limited, London.

Redford, K., and G. da Fonseca. 1986. The role of gallery forests in the zoogeography of the Cerrado's non-volant mammalian fauna. *Biotropica* 18 (2): 126-135.

Reed, D. 1981. Mule deer behavior at a highway underpass exit. *Journal of Wildlife Management* 45: 542-543.

Reed, D., T. Pojar, and T. Woodard. 1974. Use of one-way gates by mule deer. *Journal of Wildlife Management* 38: 9-15.

_____. 1974. Mule deer responses to deer guards. *Journal of Range Management* 27 (2): 111-113.

Reed, D., T. Woodward, and T. Pojar. 1975. Behavioral response of mule deer to a highway underpass. *Journal of Wildlife Management* 39: 361-367.

Ride, W. 1975. Towards an integrated system: A study of selection and acquisition of national parks and nature reserves in western Australia. In F. Fenner, ed. A national system of ecological reserves in Australia. Report 19. Australian Academy of Science, Canberra, Australia.

Risser, P., J. Karr, and R. Forman. 1984. Landscape ecology, directions and approaches. Proceedings of a workshop held at Allerton Park, Illinois. Special Publication No. 2. Illinois Natural History Survey, Champaign, Illinois.

Robbins, C. 1979. Effect of forest fragmentation on bird communities. In R. DeGraaf and K. Evans, eds. Management of north central and northeastern forests for nongame birds. Forest Service General Technical Report NC-51. U.S. Department of Agriculture, Washington, D.C.

Rogers, L. 1987. Factors influencing dispersal in black bear. In B. Chepko-Sade and Z. Tang Talpin, eds. Mammalian dispersal patterns. University of Chicago Press, Chicago.

Rubin, B., and G. Emmerich, Jr. 1981. Refining the delineation of environmental corridors in southeastern Wisconsin. Technical Record Bibliography 4 (2): 1-21. Southeastern Wisconsin Regional Planning Commission, Waukesha, Wisconsin.

Salwasser, H., C. Schonewald-Cox, and R. Baker. 1987. The role of interagency cooperation in managing for viable populations. In M. Soule, ed. Viable populations for conservation. Cambridge University Press, New York.

Sanderson, G. 1966. The study of mammal movements—a review. *Journal of Wildlife Management* 30 (1): 215-235.

Saunders, D. 1980. Food and movements of the short-billed form of the white-tailed black cockatoo. *Australian Wildlife Research* 7: 257-269.

Saunders, D., and J. Ingram. 1987. Factors affecting survival of breeding populations of Carnaby's cockatoo, *Calyptorhynchus funereus latirostris*, in remnants of native vegetation. In D. Saunders, G. Arnold, A. Burbidge, and A. Hopkins, eds. Nature conservation: The role of remnants of native vegetation. Surrey Beatty and Sons Pty. Limited, Chipping Norton, NSW, Australia.

Saunders, D., G. Arnold, A. Burbidge, and A. Hopkins, eds. 1987. Nature conservation: The role of remnants of native vegetation. Surrey Beatty and Sons Pty. Limited, Chipping Norton, NSW, Australia.

Schaller, G., H. Jinchu, P. Wenshi, and Z. Jing. 1985. The giant pandas of Wolong. University of Chicago Press, Chicago.

Simberloff, D. 1974. Equilibrium theory of island biogeography and ecology. *Annual Reviews of Ecology and Systematics* 5: 161-179.

Simberloff, D., and J. Cox. 1987. Consequences and costs of conservation corridors. *Conservation Biology* 1: 63-71.

Simpson, G. 1940. Mammals and land bridges. *Journal of the Washington Academy of Sciences* 30: 137-163.

_____. 1965. The geography of evolution. Chilton Books, Philadelphia.

Singer, F. 1975. Behavior of mountain goats in relation to US Highway 2, Glacier National Park, Montana. *Journal of Wildlife Management* 42: 591-597.

Singer, F., and J. Doherty. 1985. Movements and habitat use in an unhunted population of mountain goats (*Oreamnos americanus*). *Canadian Field Naturalist* 99: 205-217.

Smith, E. 1970. Green ribbons of hope/rights-of-way plantings hold promise of improving wildlife habitat. *Forests and People* 20: 22-23.

Soule, M., ed. 1986. Conservation biology: The science of scarcity and diversity. Sinauer Associates, Sunderland, Massachusetts.

_____. 1987. Viable populations for conservation. Cambridge University Press, New York.

Soule, M., D. Boulger, A. Alberts, R. Sauvajot, J. Wright,

M. Sorice, and S. Hill. 1988. Reconstructed dynamics of rapid extinctions of chaparral-requiring birds in urban habitat islands. *Conservation Biology* 2: 75-92.

Suckling, G. 1982. Value of reserved habitat for mammal conservation in plantations. *Australian Forestry* 45 (1): 19-27.

_____. 1984. Population ecology of the sugar glider, *Petaurus breviceps*, in a system of fragmented habitats. *Australian Wildlife Research* 11: 49-76.

Sumner, E. Jr. 1936. A life history of the California quail, with recommendations for conservation and management. California State Printing Office, Sacramento, California.

Tassone, J. 1981. Utility of hardwood leave strips for breeding birds in Virginia's central piedmont. Unpublished (M.S. thesis). Virginia Polytechnic Institute and State University, Blacksburg, Virginia.

Terborgh, J. 1974. Preservation of natural diversity: The problem of extinction prone species. *BioScience* 24: 715-722.

U.S. Fish and Wildlife Service. 1984. Land protection plan for lower Rio Grande Valley National Wildlife Refuge in Cameron, Hidalgo, Starr, and Willacy counties, Texas. Southwest Region Office, U.S. Fish and Wildlife Service, Albuquerque, New Mexico.

_____. 1987. Florida panther *(Felis concolor coryi)* recovery plan. Prepared for the U.S. Fish and Wildlife Service by the Florida Panther Interagency Committee, Atlanta, Georgia.

Walesh, S. 1976. Floodland management: The environmental corridor concept. Technical Record Bibliography 3 (6): 1-13. Southeastern Wisconsin Regional Planning Commission, Waukesha, Wisconsin.

Walters J., S. Hansen, J. Carter, P. Manor, and R. Blue. 1988. Long-distance dispersal of an adult red-cockaded woodpecker. *The Wilson Bulletin* 100 (3): 494-496.

Way, M. 1970. Wildlife on the motorway. *New Scientist* 47: 536-537.

Webb, S., and K. Wilkins. 1984. Historical biogeography of Florida Pleistocene mammals. In H. Genoways and M. Dawsen, eds. Contributions in Quaternary verte-brate paleontology. Carnegie Museum Special Publication 8. Pittsburgh, Pennsylvania.

Wegner, J., and G. Merriam. 1979. Movements by birds and small mammals between a wood and adjoining farmland habitats. *Journal of Applied Ecology* 16: 349-358.

Wells, J., and C. Peterson. 1987. Restless ribbons of sand, Atlantic and Gulf coastal barriers. Institute of Marine Sciences, University of North Carolina, Chapel Hill, North Carolina.

Whitcomb, R., C. Robbins, J. Lynch, B. Whitcomb, M. Klimkiewicz, and D. Bystrak. 1981. Effects of forest fragmentation on avifauna of the eastern deciduous forest. In R. Burgess and D. Sharpe, eds. Forest island dynamics in man-dominated landscapes. Springer Verlag, New York.

Wilcove, D. 1987. From fragmentation to extinction. *Natural Areas Journal* 7: 23-29.

Wilcove, D., and R. May. 1986. National park boundaries and ecological realities. *Nature* 324: 206-207.

Wilcove, D., C. McLellan, and A. Dobson. 1986. Habitat fragmentation in the temperate zone. In M. Soule, ed. Conservation biology: The science of scarcity and diversity. Sinauer Associates, Sunderland, Massachusetts.

Wilcox, B. 1980. Insular ecology and conservation. In M. Soule and F. Wilcox, eds. Conservation biology: An evolutionary ecological perspective. Sinauer Associates, Sunderland, Massachusetts.

Wilcox, B., and D. Murphy. 1985. Conservation strategy: The effects of fragmentation on extinction. *American Naturalist* 125: 879-887.

Wilson, E., and E. Willis. 1975. Applied biogeography. In M. Cody and J. Diamond, eds. Ecology and evolution of communities. Harvard University Press, Cambridge, Massachusetts.

Winston, M. 1987. The biology of the honey bee. Harvard University Press, Cambridge, Massachusetts.

Wooding, J., and J. Brady. 1986. Black bear roadkills in Florida. In press. *Proceedings of the Annual Conference of the Southeastern Association of Fish and Wildlife Agencies* 41.

The Thin Green Line

By Aubrey Stephen Johnson

Riparian Corridors and Endangered Species in Arizona and New Mexico

"At the heart of the desert there is no drought, there is only an occasional mitigation of dryness."
—Walter Prescott Webb (in Sheridan 1981)

Strictly speaking, the word "drought" should not be a part of the vocabulary of anyone living in the arid Southwest. To even use the word denotes a profound lack of understanding of one's own home. This is particularly true for Arizona and New Mexico, where aridity is the norm and water the great exception. The truth of this is apparent almost anywhere when one takes the time to consider the native plants and animals of these arid lands. Nearly all of them reflect in their overall physiology and behavior the reality of an ecosystem where rains are infrequent but often torrential. In such a "boom and bust" ecosystem, native life forms must take advantage of water when it is available, yet continue to function when normality returns.

The plants of the Sonoran desert, for example, often exhibit such characteristics as small leaves (or no leaves), green bark, thorns, deep (or shallow) roots, and other adaptations to obtain water, limit evaporation, and discourage consumption by animals. Aestivation, or heat-induced torpor, is a similar adaptation for many animal species. Among the most numerous of the desert vertebrates are the reptiles, where scales and leathery eggs serve moisture-conserving functions. Here predators hunt their prey as much for their store of water as for their protein (Arizona-Sonora Desert Museum 1987).

A Stream in the Desert

In such habitats, where 99 percent of the land surface may be brown and hot for much of the year, any surface streams are truly linear oases of green and marvelous concentrations of living things. In this land of extremes, healthy riparian areas are critical moderating factors, essential to the long-term health of entire watersheds. They absorb the rare but often heavy rains and release the water slowly over time, often preventing what otherwise would be destructive floods. When aridity returns to the surrounding lands, the streams continue to flow and to nourish life.

To really experience the wonder of a stream in the desert, one should visit southern Arizona or New Mexico in the summer, when the heat is a tremendous force, dominating everything. For maximum effect, the stream should be several miles away, and one should walk. Long before the stream is seen, flights of mourning doves to and from its waters will often tell of its presence. The dry and rattling flight of dragonflies may be seen, along with arrow-straight flights of honeybees and hovering millions of other insects. Early in the day and at dusk, the air near the stream will be filled with birdsong. The margins of the stream will often be a registry of the tracks of local residents that may include deer, javelina, coati, and even an occasional mountain lion. Such an experience is worth a hundred books that chronicle the harshness of the desert.

One of the most striking features of a stream in the desert is the abruptness of the transition from aridity to moisture. In the Sonoran desert, for example, it is possible to sit in the shade of a giant saguaro cactus while one's feet are soaking in a stream. With a little searching, one may find a kangaroo rat that never drinks living a few yards from a leopard frog dependent on pools of permanent water. They are both members of the Sonoran desert community yet live their lives almost as separately as if they lived on different worlds.

Riparian Ecosystems in the Arid Southwest

The desert stream is just one example of what is now recognized as the premier biological resource in the entire arid Southwest: riparian ecosystems. These critical areas are diverse in their characteristics but can generally be defined as including "vegetation, habitats, or ecosystems that are associated with bodies of water (streams or lakes) or are dependent on the existence of perennial, intermittent, or ephemeral surface or subsurface water drainage" (Arizona Riparian Council 1986). This definition is very different from the traditional description of "wetlands" used by the U.S. Fish and Wildlife Service for the remainder of the

In this land of extremes, any surface streams are truly linear oases of green and marvelous concentrations of living things.

country. While Arizona and other arid southwestern states do have some wetlands that qualify under the national definition, such areas are a small minority of the very important lands covered under the broader definition crafted by the Arizona Riparian Council.

In much of Arizona and New Mexico, the majority of riparian areas are ephemeral streams, running only a few months, weeks, or days each year. Even when dry for several consecutive years, these areas can always be identified by vegetation that is very different from the surrounding lands. Native Americans like the Apache appreciated the importance of such "dry" areas, calling them hassayampas, or "rivers which run upside down" (Arizona Nature Conservancy 1987a). The present-day Hassayampa River near Wickenburg, Arizona, is well named, since it runs "right-side-up" for only a small portion of its total length with the rest underground and betrayed only by the vegetation it supports.

Today's riparian areas are only remnants of what was a much wetter landscape just over one million years ago, the most recent time when the Sonoran and Chihuahuan deserts last expanded. It is estimated that 15 to 20 separate ice ages have caused expansion and contraction of both woodlands and deserts over the past two million years in today's Southwest (Arizona-Sonora Desert Museum 1987).

The much wetter and more extensive habitats of yesterday are probably one of the chief reasons for the extreme dependence of native wildlife species on the remaining riparian areas that exist today in the arid Southwest. Such concentrations of life are particularly striking in Arizona and New Mexico, where about 80 percent of all vertebrates are dependent upon riparian habitat for at least a portion of their life cycles. More than half of all such species cannot survive without access to riparian areas. Another 30 percent would experience declines in population without adequate riparian habitat as a part of their total habitat (Hubbard 1971; Arizona Game and Fish Department 1988; New Mexico Department of Game and Fish 1985).

Threatened Habitats and Endangered Species

Over the last century, Arizona and New Mexico are estimated to have lost 90 percent of their original riparian ecosystems (Arizona State Parks 1988). It is not surprising that these scarce riparian habitats, never comprising more than one to two percent of the total land surface even during pre-settlement times, now shelter the rarest natural community in North America: the Fremont cottonwood/Gooding willow forests. According to the Arizona Nature Conservancy (1987b), "fewer than 20 occurrences remain. Only five of the 20 are extensive. Covering less than .001 percent of Arizona's land area, cottonwood/willow forests are North America's rarest forest type."

The cottonwood/willow forests that remain are home for more than 100 state and federally listed threatened and endangered species in both Arizona and New Mexico. Some of these are the river otter, ocelot, bald eagle, gray hawk, common blackhawk, Bell's vireo, and American redstart. In the streams that sustain these forests were found many of Arizona's 32 species of fish in pre-settlement times. Today, five are gone from the state, and 21 of the remaining 27 are either officially listed as threatened or endangered or being considered for listing.

Cottonwood-lined streams such as Arizona's Aravaipa Creek are also visited frequently by desert bighorn sheep, mountain lions, and even the rare jaguar. The grizzly bear, now extinct in the area, was very dependent on the herbaceous vegetation found there, even though it is not considered a riparian species. Many of the old hunting records of dead grizzlies confirm that they spent much time in and near riparian areas (Brown 1985).

Other vegetative habitats associated with the presence of water are also rare in Arizona.

The desert stream is just one example of what is now recognized as the premier biological resource in the entire arid Southwest: riparian ecosystems.

Mesquite bosques (forests) are the fourth rarest of the 104 plant community types identified in the United States. Cienegas (wet marshes) have declined from 50 separate sites described by early Arizona explorers to only 15 today (Arizona Nature Conservancy 1987b). Of those that remain, several are threatened by overgrazing and groundwater pumping. Only one is protected, now a Nature Conservancy Preserve.

Impacts of Human Settlement on Arid Lands

It was predictable that the Anglo settlement of the Southwest would lead to the destruction of the eons-long balance between the land and the living creatures dependent upon it, humans included. There are many reasons for this, all centering on the remarkable lack of understanding of a new environmental reality prevailing beyond the 100th meridian of the United States, west of which rainfall averages less than 20 inches per year.

Americans in the middle and late 1800s were determined to "turn half a continent into something they were used to. It was a doomed effort" (Reisner 1986). For many, the baggage carried by their wagon trains, the seeds and the plows, would be negated by the baggage they carried in their minds. "Rain would follow the plow," they believed, making the land like that from which they had come.

Nowhere is the contrast more extreme between the green East and the brown West than in the arid Southwest. During the thousands of years before the invasion of Europeans, human settlements tended to cluster along the region's streams. Even today, there remain plentiful signs of extensive prehistoric irrigation ditches. At the confluence of the Gila, Salt, and Verde Rivers, for example, where Phoenix now stands, the Hohokam civilization thrived for 1,000 years, reaching an estimated population of up to 400,000 before disappearing about A.D. 1400. With plenty of water, the reason for its disappearance may have been the salt build-up that usually accompanies flood irrigation methods. Little remains today but the name, a Pima Indian word meaning "those who have gone." The first Anglo settlers to arrive in the 1830s and 1840s found nothing but small groups of nomadic hunting and gathering peoples scattered thinly over the land. No purely agricultural cultures existed; extensive human manipulation of the ecosystem had stopped more than four centuries before (Arizona State Parks 1988; Reisner 1986).

Like the remnant Indian peoples inhabiting the Southwest when they arrived, the new settlers also tended to cluster along the infrequent surface waters. Correctly perceiving that ownership of the scarce surface water meant control of the surrounding lands without the necessity for extensive land purchases, early settlers concentrated on homesteading the riparian areas of New Mexico and Arizona. Brown (1985) tells of the taking of the lands where water could be found: "By 1912, when Arizona and New Mexico attained statehood, the Southwest had been thoroughly settled. Almost every live stream, every arable piece of flat ground, every meadow possessed a ranch or farm. Use of the range was universal, and there were more people in the mountains than there are now."

The arid upland watersheds were useless to anyone without ownership of the limited surface waters. These dry lands, through default, became our public lands. But ownership of the water meant that these huge expanses of federal lands remained under the control of a few ranchers. In effect, the federal lands were de facto private lands (Brown 1985). The passage of the Taylor Grazing Act in 1934 legalized this arrangement and made ownership of some private property a requirement for leasing federal grazing land. In portions of the arid Southwest administered by the Bureau of Land Management, no ownership of land is even required. One has only to own the water rights.

The land generally remains far below its ecological potential to support maximum wildlife diversity. This is particularly true for riparian areas.

One Bite at a Time: Grazing Impacts on Riparian Ecosystems

Without question, riparian zones are the most impacted land forms in the Southwest (Arizona Game and Fish Department 1988; New Mexico Department of Game and Fish 1985). Groundwater pumping, overgrazing by livestock, dam construction, water diversions, flood control measures, conversions to pasture and croplands, and road construction have decimated riparian ecosystems. The physical disturbances caused by man's activities have also allowed widespread invasion of exotic plants such as the tamarisk into many riparian areas, making regeneration of native vegetation more difficult. The tamarisk, imported from the Middle East as an ornamental windbreak, is a particularly aggressive invader species and is very difficult to eradicate once established (Arizona State Parks 1988).

Of these negative impacts, the oldest and most widespread is livestock grazing (Fradkin 1979). The introduction of a large exotic ungulate into an ecosystem that in recent geologic times never supported anything as large as a cow was an ecological disaster. Native ungulates such as the deer, pronghorn, and bighorn sheep consume far less than the 12,000 pounds of plants eaten annually by a single cow. In addition, the cow is a "wide-spectrum" feeder, meaning that it can eat almost anything, particularly when under environmental stress (Wagner 1978). With many areas now devoid of native perennial grasses, today's cattle must be both grazers and browsers, bringing them into direct competition with deer, pronghorns, javelina, and other native herbivores (Nowakowski et al. 1982). Cattle grazing in an arid land characterized by a boom-and-bust regime has had predictable and long-term consequences, particularly for riparian areas.

Until the introduction of windmills and stock tanks about 1900, cattle grazing was confined near the permanent streams. (Cattle rarely travel distances greater than two miles from water and only lightly graze areas farther than one mile from permanent water.) Using early data from Arizona cattle numbers reported for tax purposes, it is now believed that about 380,000 cattle grazed along and near the permanent streams of southern Arizona during each of the five years prior to 1893 (Arizona State Parks 1988).

Much of the destruction we see today is a legacy of those early years. Now, even with the use of developed water supplies that allow cattle to utilize a vastly expanded area, only about 180,000 cattle graze the same land. Even so, it is well documented that grazing levels continue to negatively impact the arid West (Wald and Alberswerth 1985; Sheridan 1981). While some recovery has occurred in the last 50 years on the arid uplands, the land generally remains far below its ecological potential to support maximum wildlife diversity. This is particularly true for riparian areas (Platts 1979; Elmore and Beschta 1987; Nowakowski et al. 1982).

When riparian habitats are overgrazed, vegetation is removed from stream sides, leading to erosion and stream sedimentation. Trampling of denuded streambanks leads to channel widening and consequent water temperature increases. Stream pollution results from cattle wastes. The extent of riparian abuse is often so severe that both water and associated vegetation disappear entirely, transforming a perennial, wooded stream into another barren arroyo. Even where a few adult cottonwood trees remain, there are often no seedlings that escape the cow's voracious appetite, nothing to indicate a hundred years of reproductive effort (Davis 1986).

In June 1988, the General Accounting Office released a report on the condition of the nation's riparian areas on public rangelands, finding that "poorly managed livestock grazing is the major

Tens of thousands of miles of streambanks throughout the West are denuded and degraded. The prognosis is not encouraging.

cause of degraded riparian habitat on federal rangelands." The report concludes that in general there are no technical barriers to riparian restoration but that politics are interfering with compliance with federal laws and policies requiring protection and restoration of these vital areas. In addition, the General Accounting Office found that budget cuts have greatly decreased the number of government biologists and other employees available to carry out restoration work in riparian areas. The result is that tens of thousands of miles of streambanks throughout the West are denuded and degraded. The prognosis for the future is not encouraging: "At the current pace, it will probably take several decades, and in some places even longer, before most riparian areas are restored to good condition."

Declining Diversity on Public Lands

The 1988 General Accounting Office report is only the latest in a long series of writings detailing the decline in ecosystem diversity on our public lands and the failure of the federal land management agencies to do their jobs as required by numerous laws. In "The Eating of the West," Philip Fradkin (1979) says that "the impact of countless hooves and mouths over the years has done more to alter the type of vegetation and landforms of the West than all the water projects, stripmines, powerplants, freeways, and subdivision developments combined. The changes, in most cases, are irrevocable."

According to the Natural Resources Law Institute (1986) of the Lewis and Clark Law School:

Figure 1. Riparian Habitats and Locations of Species Rare or Endangered in Arizona.

ARIZONA

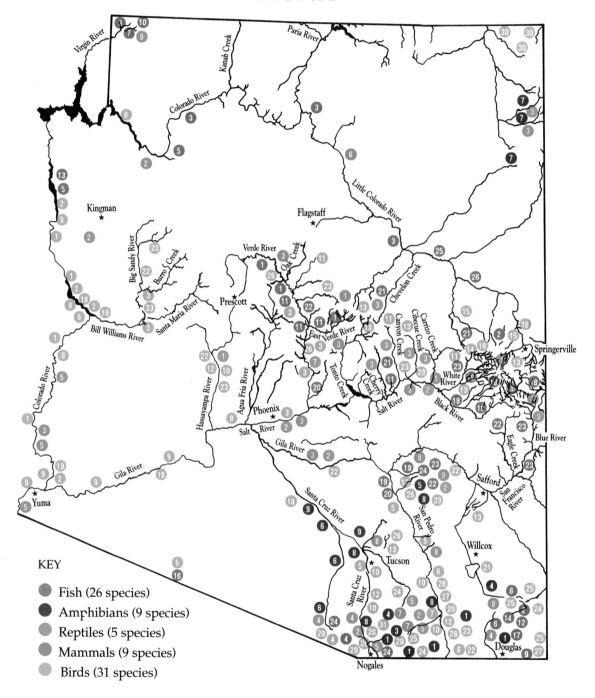

KEY

- ● Fish (26 species)
- ● Amphibians (9 species)
- ● Reptiles (5 species)
- ● Mammals (9 species)
- ● Birds (31 species)

ARIZONA

Reflecting its varied topography, climate, geology, and evolutionary history, Arizona has a great diversity of habitats. The state has more than 200 major types of plant communities and aquatic features and more than 800 species of vertebrate wildlife.

According to the working draft of *Threatened Native Wildlife in Arizona* (Arizona Game and Fish Department 1988), 81 of Arizona's 115 threatened vertebrate species are either closely associated with or completely dependent upon riparian habitat; 70 percent of those species require riparian habitat in order to survive.

In interpreting the map showing the locations of the 81 threatened vertebrate species in Arizona, the following cautions apply:

1) The small scale of the map means that habitat locations are only approximate.

2) Many riparian areas are too small to be shown except by location of the species concerned.

3) Many species remain very poorly known and have not been completely surveyed.

4) Species of widespread distribution may still occur in very low numbers overall.

5) The majority of the streams shown flow perennially for only a small portion of their length. Many other formerly perennial streams are now mostly ephemeral due to diversions, impoundments, water pumping, and destruction of watersheds by overgrazing.

● FISH

1) Gila trout
2) Arizona stoneroller
3) Humpback chub
4) Sonora chub
5) Bonytail chub
6) Taqui chub
7) Virgin roundtail chub
8) Virgin spinedace
9) Yaqui shiner
10) Woundfin
11) Colorado squawfish
12) Yaqui sucker
13) Razorback sucker
14) Yaqui catfish
15) Desert pupfish
16) Quitobaquito pupfish
17) Yaqui topminnow
18) Apache trout
19) Gila chub
20) Colorado roundtail chub
21) Little Colorado spinedace
22) Spikedace
23) Loach minnow
24) Gila topminnow
25) Little Colorado sucker
26) Zuni Mountain sucker

● AMPHIBIANS

1) Huachuca tiger salamander
2) Barking frog
3) Tarahumara frog
4) Plains leopard frog
5) Chiricahua leopard frog
6) Northern casque-headed frog
7) Northern leopard frog
8) Lowland leopard frog
9) Great Plains narrow-mouthed toad

● REPTILES

1) Arizona skink
2) Mexican garter snake
3) Narrow-headed garter snake
4) Brown vine snake
5) Arizona ridge-nosed rattlesnake

● MAMMALS

1) Water shrew
2) Hualapai Mexican vole
3) Southwestern river otter
4) Ocelot
5) Yuma puma
6) Navajo Mexican vole
7) Arizona shrew
8) Red bat
9) Spotted bat

● BIRDS

1) Great egret
2) Black rail
3) Bald eagle
4) Masked bobwhite
5) Ferruginous pygmy owl
6) Willow flycatcher
7) Buff-breasted flycatcher
8) Snowy egret
9) Yuma clapper rail
10) Gray hawk
11) Osprey
12) Yellow-billed cuckoo
13) Spotted owl
14) Veery
15) Gray catbird
16) American redstart
17) Clark's phoebe
18) Least bittern
19) American bittern
20) Black-bellied whistling duck
21) Snowy plover
22) Mississippi kite
23) Common black-hawk
24) Elegant trogon
25) Violet-crowned hummingbird
26) Belted kingfisher
27) Thick-billed kingbird
28) Tropical kingbird
29) Rose-throated becard
30) Black-billed magpie
31) Black-capped gnatcatcher

Figure 2. Riparian Habitats and Locations of Species Rare or Endangered in New Mexico.

NEW MEXICO

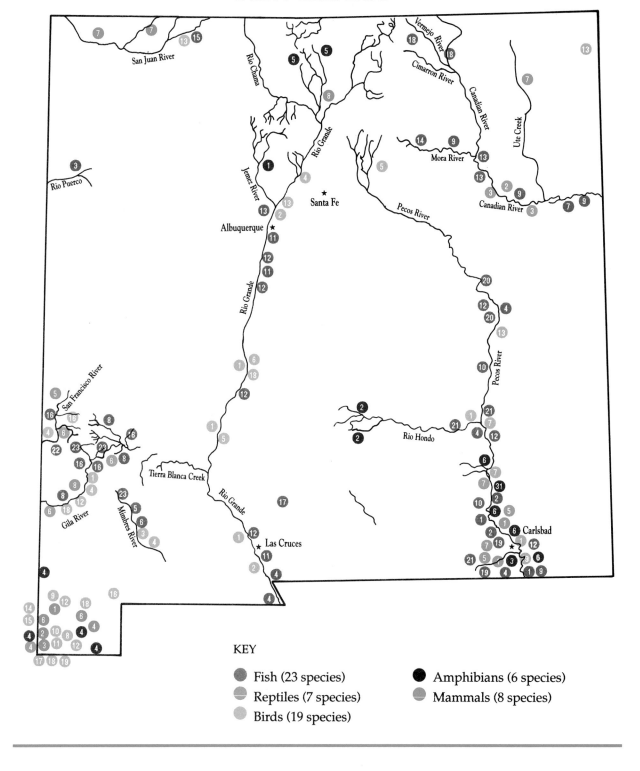

KEY

- ● Fish (23 species)
- ● Reptiles (7 species)
- ● Birds (19 species)
- ● Amphibians (6 species)
- ● Mammals (8 species)

NEW MEXICO

According to the *Handbook of Species Endangered in New Mexico* (New Mexico Department of Game and Fish 1985), 69 of New Mexico's 94 threatened vertebrate species are either closely associated with or completely dependent upon riparian habitat; 73 percent of those species require riparian habitats in order to survive.

In interpreting the map showing the location of the 69 threatened species in New Mexico, the following cautions apply:

1) The small scale of the map means that habitat locations are only approximate.

2) Many riparian areas are too small to be shown except by location of the species concerned.

3) Many species remain very poorly known and have not been completely surveyed.

4) Species of widespread distribution may still occur in very low numbers overall.

5) The majority of the streams shown flow perennially for only a small portion of their length. Many other formerly perennial streams are now mostly ephemeral due to diversions, impoundments, water pumping, and destruction of watersheds by overgrazing.

● FISH

1) Blue sucker
2) Gray redhorse
3) Zuni Mountain sucker
4) Mexican tetra
5) Roundtail chub
6) Chihuahua chub
7) Speckled dace
8) Spikedace
9) Arkansas River shiner
10) Silverband shiner
11) Bluntnose shiner
12) Silvery minnow
13) Suckermouth minnow
14) Southern redbelly dace
15) Colorado River squawfish
16) Loach minnow
17) White Sands pupfish
18) Brook stickleback
19) Greenthroat darter
20) Bigscale logperch
21) Pecos gambusia
22) Gila topminnow
23) Gila trout

● AMPHIBIANS

1) Jemez Mountain salamander
2) Sacramento Mountain salamander
3) Eastern barking frog
4) Colorado River toad
5) Western boreal toad
6) Blanchard's cricket frog

● REPTILES

1) Texas slider turtle
2) Western spiny softshell turtle
3) Smooth softshell turtle
4) Mountain skink
5) Plain-bellied water snake
6) Narrow-headed garter snake
7) Pecos western ribbon snake

● MAMMALS

1) Arizona shrew
2) Southern yellow bat
3) Western mastiff bat
4) Southern pocket gopher
5) Arizona montane vole
6) Coatimundi
7) Mink
8) River otter

● BIRDS

1) Olivaceous cormorant
2) Mississippi kite
3) Gray hawk
4) Black hawk
5) Bald eagle
6) Whooping crane
7) Least tern
8) Violet-crowned hummingbird
9) White-eared hummingbird
10) Broad-billed hummingbird
11) Coppery-tailed trogon
12) Gila woodpecker
13) Red-headed woodpecker
14) Thick-billed kingbird
15) Sulphur-bellied flycatcher
16) Buff-breasted flycatcher
17) Beardless flycatcher
18) Bell's vireo
19) Varied bunting

Comparison of Threatened and Endangered Species in Arizona and New Mexico

Despite the fact that Arizona and New Mexico are similar in many ways, it is interesting to note that relatively few of the threatened species occur in both states. Of the total of 149 threatened vertebrate species, only 17 (about 11 percent) are found in both Arizona and New Mexico. As might be expected because of their general lack of mobility, the reptile and amphibian groups contain the fewest species found in both states, while the birds and fish are the most widespread. However, a number of the reptile and amphibian species in the two states are closely related, perhaps evolving from a common ancestor. The fact that they "split off" is yet another indication of the long distances between riparian habitats and the effects of such isolation on the development of new species over time.

The Taylor [Grazing] Act still forms the basis for livestock grazing on public lands, but it is incapable of remedying ecological damage caused by decades of abusive range use, particularly damage to riparian and aquatic ecosystems requiring years of livestock exclusion to regenerate. Although the Act ostensibly regulated grazing for the purpose of protecting the land, its permit system and its preferences created a class of entrenched resource users whose interests did not coincide with fish habitat rehabilitation.

Riparian Habitats and Endangered Species

While many books and articles refer to the decline of species diversity, none has examined the link between riparian habitat and the number of rare and endangered species dependent upon such habitats. Figures 1 and 2 list the rare and endangered vertebrates of Arizona and New Mexico, with their known habitats shown on small-scale maps of the two states. In general, it was found that approximately 70 percent of these species occur in and near the riparian zones of Arizona and New Mexico (Arizona Game and Fish Department 1988; New Mexico Department of Game and Fish 1985).

In plotting the locations for each species, it became apparent that it is not necessary to specifically outline the riparian areas: The habitat locations of the rare and endangered species are all that is needed to identify these critical areas. If we are to address the recovery of such species, it is obvious that riparian areas must be protected from further abuse and that active efforts at recovery must begin as soon as possible.

The recent emphasis and concern about riparian areas as critical ecosystems deserving recovery and protection comes at a time when the Endangered Species Act appears to be less and less capable of doing the job for which it was designed. It is increasingly clear that the strategy of addressing endangered species one at a time, as outlined by the act, is ineffective. More than 500 species are now listed as threatened or endangered in the United States alone, with an additional 3,900 or so identified as species deserving of listing or species

Riparian areas are often critical corridors that allow wildlife movement from one important habitat to another. Without such corridors, many isolated wildlife habitats would be too small to support the maximum diversity of species.

for which more data is needed. With only 239 recovery plans approved (through the end of fiscal year 1988) since the Endangered Species Act became law 15 years ago, we are falling farther and farther behind. An additional problem, given level funding for the program, is the inevitable dilution of both personnel and funding with each new species listed (Scott et al. 1988). Even with the 1988 reauthorization and strengthening of the act, which now provides for much higher funding levels through 1992, recovery plans will remain unable to keep up with the accelerating number of species in jeopardy from lost or degraded habitat.

Preventing Endangerment

If the effort to save and recover endangered species is not to deteriorate even further into mere efforts to document their loss through the listing process, changes need to be made. One of the more promising possibilities is to shift "some of our focus on individual species to a more broad-based ecosystem approach aimed at preventing species from becoming endangered" (Scott et al. 1988). The biological importance of riparian areas, coupled with their potential to respond quickly to protection (Platts 1979; General Accounting Office

1988; Voight 1976), makes them obvious candidates for emphasis in the drive to ensure the integrity of existing natural communities and ecosystems.

Finally, riparian areas are often critical corridors that allow wildlife movement from one important habitat to another. Without such corridors, many isolated wildlife habitats would be too small to support the maximum diversity of species. Without the genetic interchange made possible by wildlife movement corridors, these human-caused "island habitats" would inevitably contain far fewer species and far less diversity of life.

Two decades ago, ecologists Robert MacArthur and E. O. Wilson (1967) synthesized their own and others' observations into a new theory of island biogeography. They found that an island reduced in size by one-half will eventually lose about 90 percent of its original species. With ever-proliferating barriers to wildlife movement such as roads, powerlines, and canals, man is steadily shrinking existing wildlife habitat into ever smaller islands. Since this is a trend not likely to be reversed, the corridor effect of riparian habitat linking such islands will assume greater and greater importance in the future.

Today, we find ourselves in a position never before attained by any species on earth. We have so influenced the natural ecosystems of the planet that thousands of species of plants and animals are now responding to changes caused by humankind. Our most innocent act carries with it unforeseen consequences. In learning to use our strengths to remake the world into a human-centered community, we also have greatly simplified our environment and only lately have begun to suspect that both we and our world are more vulnerable as a result.

In adopting new approaches to maintain the diversity of life, we also are helping ourselves. There is no substitute for diversity, nothing to take the place of the millions of species whose lives, in concert with our own, sustain the thin film of life on earth.

Aubrey Stephen Johnson has served as Southwest regional representative for Defenders of Wildlife since 1973. He earned his bachelor's and master's degrees in biology, history, and education at the University of Arizona. He has written many newspaper and journal articles on wildlife habitat protection in the Southwest, with particular emphasis on grazing policies and public land management to restore riparian habitats for endangered species and other wildlife.

Selected Bibliography

Arizona Game and Fish Department. 1988. Threatened native wildlife of Arizona. Draft. Arizona Game and Fish Department, Phoenix.

Arizona Nature Conservancy. 1987a. Newsletter (Spring). Arizona Nature Conservancy Office, Tucson.

_____. 1987b. Streams of life—a conservation campaign. Arizona Nature Conservancy Office, Tucson.

Arizona State Parks. 1988. Arizona wetlands priority plan. Arizona State Parks, Phoenix.

Arizona-Sonora Desert Museum. 1987. *Sonorensis* (Fall). Arizona-Sonora Desert Museum, Tucson.

Brown, D. 1985. The grizzly in the Southwest. University of Arizona Press, Tucson.

Bureau of Land Management. 1974. Effects of livestock grazing on wildlife, watershed, recreation and other resource values in Nevada. Internal report. Bureau of Land Management, Reno, Nevada.

_____. 1987. Public lands statistics, 1987. U.S. Department of the Interior, Washington, D.C.

Davis, J.W. 1986. Options for managing livestock and riparian habitat. Forest Service, U.S. Department of Agriculture, Washington, D.C.

Elmore, W., and R.L. Beschta. 1987. Riparian areas: Perceptions in management. *Rangelands* 9 (December): 260-70.

Fradkin, P. 1979. The eating of the West. *Audubon* 81 (January): 94-121.

General Accounting Office. 1988. Public rangelands: Some riparian areas restored but widespread improvement will be slow. General Accounting Office, U.S. Government, Washington, D.C.

Hubbard, J.P. 1971. The summer birds of the Gila Valley, New Mexico. *Nemouria:* Occasional papers of the Delaware Museum of Natural History, No. 2. Delaware Museum of Natural History, Wilmington.

MacArthur, R., and E.O. Wilson. 1967. The theory of island biogeography. Princeton University Press, Princeton, New Jersey.

Natural Resources Law Institute. 1986. Livestock grazing in riparian zones: Ensuring fishery protection in federal land management. *Anadromous Fish Law Memo* (October). Lewis and Clark Law School, Portland, Oregon.

New Mexico Department of Game and Fish. 1985. Handbook of species endangered in New Mexico. New Mexico Department of Game and Fish, Santa Fe.

Nowakowski, N.A., et al. 1982. Livestock-wildlife interactions in the Southwest. Forest Service (Southwest Region), U.S. Department of Agriculture, Albuquerque, New Mexico.

Platts, W.S. 1979. Livestock grazing and riparian/stream ecosystems—an overview. Forest Service, U.S. Department of Agriculture, Washington, D.C.

Reisner, M. 1986. Cadillac desert. Penguin Books, New York.

Scott, J.M., B. Csuti, K. Smith, J.E. Estes, and S. Caicco. 1988. Beyond endangered species: An integrated strategy for the preservation of biological diversity. *Endangered Species Update* 5 (August): 43-48.

Sheridan, D. 1981. Desertification of the United States. Council on Environmental Quality, Washington, D.C.

Voight, W. 1976. Public grazing lands. Rutgers Press, New Brunswick, New Jersey.

Wagner, F.H. 1978. Grazing and the livestock industry. In Wildlife and America. Council on Environmental Quality, Washington, D.C.

Wald, J., and D. Alberswerth. 1985. Our ailing public rangelands: Condition report—1985. Natural Resources Defense Council and National Wildlife Federation, Washington, D.C.

Saving Endangered Species

By Ginger Merchant Meese

Implementing the Endangered Species Act

The nation's most important wildlife legislation, the Endangered Species Act of 1973, was reaffirmed and strengthened just in time to celebrate its fifteenth anniversary. In October 1988, at the end of the 100th Congress, the act was reauthorized through 1992 with increased funding and stronger provisions. Following a four-year battle over numerous weakening amendments proposed by special interests, legislators in both houses of Congress finally adopted a strengthened Endangered Species Act by overwhelming majority. In so doing, the Congress reflected nationwide support for protecting the diversity of wild fauna and flora.

During the Reagan administration, the Congress and the American people demonstrated far greater support for the conservation of threatened and endangered species than did the administration and the federal agencies with programs affecting species and their habitats. Despite increased understanding of the magnitude of threats to the survival of wild species and despite the great number of plants and animals already known to be in danger, the administration systematically under-mined protections potentially afforded by the Endangered Species Act.

Financial and professional resources allocated to endangered species work were reduced. Conflicts with development projects and commercial activities were minimized. As a consequence, both domestic and foreign species suffered. The success stories for a small number of recovering species are offset by nearly a decade of too little help for the vast majority of threatened and endangered animals and plants.

The Endangered Species Act alone cannot preserve the natural diversity of wildlife. It is clear that the destruction of vast natural areas and the degradation of the environment that threatens all species including our own require more than this one act to correct. Yet the Endangered Species Act is central to the effort. If implemented as Congress intended, the act is a powerful but equitable means of preventing extinctions and promoting recovered populations of plants and animals.

The 1988 reauthorization gives the Bush administration the means with which to stem the rising tide of extinctions. The new administration has the opportunity to provide the leadership on endangered wildlife sought by the Congress and the American people and to develop broader initiatives to prevent endangerment of species through habitat preservation.

Basic Provisions of the Endangered Species Act

The Endangered Species Act of 1973 gives the Secretary of the Interior and the Secretary of Commerce the principal responsibility for implementing and enforcing its provisions. Day-to-day tasks are carried out by the Interior Department's U.S. Fish and Wildlife Service and the Commerce Department's National Marine Fisheries Service. In general, the latter has responsibility for marine species and the former for all others. Sea turtles come under the jurisdiction of both agencies. Certain marine mammals—the polar bear, sea otter, walrus, manatee, and dugong—are the responsibility of the Fish and Wildlife Service.

The act gives the Secretary of Agriculture responsibility for enforcing provisions pertaining to the importation or exportation of terrestrial plant species, a responsibility delegated to the Animal and Plant Health Inspection Service. The 1988 amendments provide for the Secretary of the Interior to share responsibility for controlling international trafficking in rare plants.

The Endangered Species Act establishes a comprehensive program to conserve those species that are determined to be endangered (in danger of extinction in all or a significant portion of their ranges) or threatened (likely to become endangered). Any species or subspecies of plant or animal may be eligible for protection, including species found outside the United States. Distinct populations of vertebrate animals also may be protected under the act.

The first step in protection is official listing on the "Endangered and Threatened Wildlife and Plants" list maintained by the Fish and Wildlife Service. Listing is critical: It brings the basic protective provisions of the act into force. Species that potentially qualify for listing are identified as "candidates" by the administering agencies, or they may be the subject of petitions from state or local governments, private citizens, or organizations.

Listing is a formal process with opportunities for public review and comment. The process includes a status review, a proposal to list, and a final listing decision published in the *Federal Register.* To the "maximum extent prudent and determinable," the "critical habitat" on which a species depends is to be designated at the time of listing. This is habitat that is essential to the survival and recovery of the species and may thus require special management or protection.

Once a species has been listed, its chances of survival are improved by the act's provisions for protection and recovery—but only insofar as the provisions are implemented and enforced. Key provisions include:

• "Taking" (killing, collecting, or otherwise harming) and interstate and foreign trade are generally prohibited. (Exemptions may be permitted for a limited number of special circumstances such as for scientific research or trade in captive-bred rather than wild animals.)

• All federal agencies are required to not jeopardize the continued existence of listed species or damage their critical habitat. And, further, all federal agencies are required to administer their programs in ways that will enhance the survival of endangered and threatened species.

• Recovery plans—blueprints for the survival and eventual recovery of species to viable population levels—must be prepared and implemented.

• Federal agencies are to acquire habitat essential for conserving listed species.

In addition, the act sets forth procedures and authorizes funding for cooperative efforts with

*S*pecies are not intended to remain on the threatened and endangered list permanently. The goal of the Endangered Species Act is to protect them and promote their recovery.

states and U.S. territories that have programs to conserve endangered species, if the programs meet the standards of the act. It establishes procedures for international cooperation and for implementing U.S. participation in important international treaties, including the Convention on International Trade in Endangered Species (CITES). And it provides for citizen involvement, including the right to bring lawsuits against violators of the act and the federal government.

Species are not intended to remain on the threatened and endangered list permanently. The goal of the Endangered Species Act is to protect them and promote their recovery. As a species' status improves, it can and should be reclassified—for example, from endangered to threatened—and eventually removed from the list altogether through the "delisting" process. Species may also be delisted for other reasons such as extinction or inappropriate listing.

Implementing the Endangered Species Act: 1987-88 Update

Listing of Species

In 1988 the number of species listed as threatened and endangered worldwide topped 1,000 (including full species, subspecies, and some specific populations of vertebrates). More than one half of these listed species are native to the United States

and its territories. These species are distributed unevenly throughout the nation, but all states have some resident species on the federal list (see figure 1).

As of June 30, 1988 (the most recent date for state-by-state listing information), California led the nation in federally listed species with 80. California also had the second largest number of plant

Figure 1. Number of Species[1] Listed as Threatened or Endangered in the United States by State and Territory as of June 30, 1988.[2]

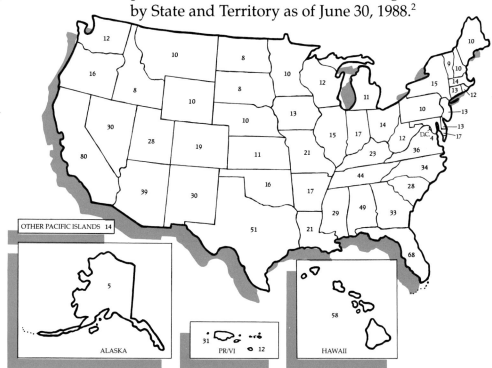

[1] Includes subspecies and some populations of vertebrates as appropriate.
[2] Counts are for current ranges only.

Source: Division of Endangered Species and Habitat Conservation, U.S. Fish and Wildlife Service, 1988.

candidate species awaiting listing. Other states with more than 50 threatened or endangered species include Florida, Hawaii, and Texas. Alaska is notable for two reasons: It has the fewest species listed as threatened or endangered (only five as of mid-1988); and 1988 marked the first listing of an Alaskan plant species—the Aleutian shield fern.

As of October 1988, a total of ten species had been delisted as extinct (six) or recovered (four). Two species familiar to the public are not represented in these figures. The American alligator, which has recovered biologically, remains on the list under the special classification "threatened by similarity of appearance" because of the difficulty in distinguishing it from the endangered American crocodile and other crocodilians worldwide. The dusky seaside sparrow, a subspecies that became extinct with the death in 1987 of its last member, "Orange Band," at Florida's Walt Disney World, has not yet been officially removed from the protected list.

In the early 1980s, the Reagan administration attempted to halt listing, including listing actions planned during the Carter administration, purportedly to emphasize recovery of species already listed. Subsequent decisions made it clear, however, that the administration's primary concern was to avoid potential conflicts with development interests. The Congress responded in 1982 amendments to the Endangered Species Act by reaffirming that listing decisions are to be based upon biological data and specifically excluding economic considerations from those decisions. The Congress also set deadlines for agency decisions on petitions to list species.

Although listing resumed, the administration delayed controversial listings within the bureaucracy and held the listing objective of the Fish and Wildlife Service to a modest 50 species a year. Species with significant potential for conflict with human activities such as the desert tortoise, the northern spotted owl, and the Louisiana black bear have been relegated to candidate status while the listing quota of 50 per year is filled through less controversial species. As table 1 shows, the Fish and Wildlife Service exceeded its quota in 1987 by nine, while delisting and reclassifying four species.

During the first half of 1988, the Fish and Wildlife Service listed only 12 species—11 plants and one mussel—despite entering the year with 49 proposed listings to finalize. The apparent decline in listing activity was due at least in part to a formal reorganization of the service in 1987, resulting in extensive shifting of personnel as program management was replaced with line-authority management. The effort to decentralize the service was completed with the transfer of most of the functions of the former Office of Endangered Species in Washington, D.C., to the regional offices. Listing and recovery activities that remained in Washington are now in one branch of the Washington Division of Endangered Species and Habitat Conservation. Responsibility for species outside the United States was transferred to the Office of the Scientific Authority (U.S. Fish and Wildlife Service 1987b).

Table 1. Number of Species[1] Listed, Reclassified, and Delisted, 1973-1988.[2]

| | Nixon | Ford | | | Carter | | | | Reagan | | | | | | | |
	1973[3]	74	75	76	77	78	79	80	81	82	83	84	85	86	87	88
Listed	402	3	9	189	20	36	68	21	4	10	23	47	60	45	59	43
Reclassified			2		1	2	1	1	1	1	1	4	1	0	3	2
Delisted						1				1	4	3	4	0	1	0

[1] Includes subspecies and some specific populations of vertebrates.

[2] Calendar years (data for 1988 through September 30).

[3] Species listed under the authority of the Endangered Species Preservation Act of 1966 and Endangered Species Conservation Act of 1969.

Source: Listing Action Summaries, Division of Endangered Species and Habitat Conservation, U.S. Fish and Wildlife Service, 1973-1988.

Reportedly, the listing process was functioning more efficiently in the summer of 1988. Final listings had picked up significantly by the end of the federal fiscal year, with 43 species added to the list as of September 30, 1988.

The National Marine Fisheries Service lists very few species. In May 1988 it proposed the Chinese river dolphin as endangered in response to a petition; in August, it published notice in the *Federal Register* of the development of its first list of candidate species that may warrant listing.

A Burgeoning Backlog of Candidate Species

Any delay in listing and consequent protection of species is doubly regrettable because so many qualifying species are already backlogged (see figure 2). Nearly twice the number of U.S. species now listed are qualified for listing but waiting to be afforded the basic protections of the Endangered Species Act. In all, more than 3,900 species in the United States are considered official candidates. Two hundred to three hundred of these species, many of them plants, may already be extinct. The large backlog and the number of possibly extinct "candidate" species indicate a serious breakdown in implementing the Endangered Species Act.

Candidate species are classified into two categories: Category one species qualify for listing based on available data; category two species require additional information as to their status. The number of candidate species backlogged for

Figure 2. Status of U.S. Animal and Plant Species: Approximate Numbers at Various Stages of Listing and Recovery as of September 30, 1988.

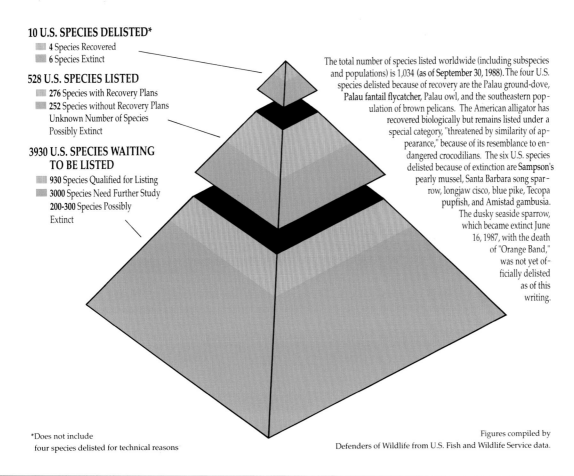

10 U.S. SPECIES DELISTED*
- **4** Species Recovered
- **6** Species Extinct

528 U.S. SPECIES LISTED
- **276** Species with Recovery Plans
- **252** Species without Recovery Plans
- Unknown Number of Species Possibly Extinct

3930 U.S. SPECIES WAITING TO BE LISTED
- **930** Species Qualified for Listing
- **3000** Species Need Further Study
- **200-300** Species Possibly Extinct

The total number of species listed worldwide (including subspecies and populations) is 1,034 (as of September 30, 1988). The four U.S. species delisted because of recovery are the Palau ground-dove, Palau fantail flycatcher, Palau owl, and the southeastern population of brown pelicans. The American alligator has recovered biologically but remains listed under a special category, "threatened by similarity of appearance," because of its resemblance to endangered crocodilians. The six U.S. species delisted because of extinction are Sampson's pearly mussel, Santa Barbara song sparrow, longjaw cisco, blue pike, Tecopa pupfish, and Amistad gambusia. The dusky seaside sparrow, which became extinct June 16, 1987, with the death of "Orange Band," was not yet officially delisted as of this writing.

*Does not include four species delisted for technical reasons

Figures compiled by Defenders of Wildlife from U.S. Fish and Wildlife Service data.

consideration continues to grow despite the removal of those added to the official list of threatened and endangered species. By 1985, 80 species had been dropped from the candidate list as extinct. Listing for other candidates did not come until they were virtually extinct. The possibly extinct candidate species pose a special problem. In part because of limited resources, the Fish and Wildlife Service is not moving to list these species or to actively search for them. The best hope for their survival is that they will be rediscovered and brought to the attention of service biologists, as happened with the running buffalo clover in 1985. Since its rediscovery, the clover has been listed, and survey work has located additional remnant populations (U.S. Fish and Wildlife Service 1987a). As a result, the species' survival and recovery potential is greatly enhanced.

Recovering Species

The protective provisions of the Endangered Species Act are designed to reduce the threats from human activities to listed species and their habitats and thus to increase the species' chances for survival. As noted earlier, the act also calls for recovery plans prepared by teams of experts to identify the information and management actions needed to prevent extinction and return a species to self-sustaining population levels. Often, cooperative efforts involving several state and federal agencies and sometimes private entities are necessary to recover a species.

In the 15-year history of the act, only five listed species have been recovered—three bird species native to the Pacific island of Palau, the brown pelican (southeastern U.S. population only), and the American alligator (which remains listed under the special category of "threatened by similarity of appearance"). A few listed species are making a strong comeback—particularly the peregrine falcon and the bald eagle, both threatened with extinction from DDT, which was banned in the early 1970s. Still others are increasing in numbers or are seeing the threats to their survival reduced—for example, the Utah prairie dog, Knowlton cactus, Gila trout, Aleutian Canada goose, and Tinian monarch flycatcher of the Mariana Islands. Fortunately, some listed plant species such as the small

The protective provisions of the Endangered Species Act are designed to reduce the threats from human activities to listed species and thus to increase the species' chances for survival.

whorled pogonia (a native orchid), the Furbish lousewort (a member of the snapdragon family), and the Rydberg milkvetch are proving to be more abundant than once believed.

Nonetheless, the recovery of species, like their listing, is seriously lagging. Through September 1988, extinctions accounted for more delistings than did recovery. And just as there are species making comebacks, there are also species on the list such as the red-cockaded woodpecker and desert tortoise that are continuing to decline, species such as the Alabama cavefish that are in immediate danger of extinction, and species such as the Palos Verdes blue butterfly and some of the Hawaiian forest birds that are believed to be extinct.

All too often, the major causes of a species' decline are not identified or alleviated until the species is on the very brink of extinction and its plight becomes popularized. In some cases, costly captive breeding of the last individuals is the only hope for survival of a species. In the late 1970s, red wolves were removed from the wild, and in 1987, the last black-footed ferrets and California condors were captured for captive-breeding purposes. The ultimate goal of these efforts is to return the species to the wild through reintroductions to suitable habitat. In order to accomplish this, however, habitat capable of sustaining the species must be available. In some cases, it may no longer be.

The return of the red wolf to the Southeast has begun—marking the first reintroduction in North America of an animal extinct in the wild. In the spring of 1988, the first wild pups were born to captive-bred adult wolves that had been released in Alligator River National Wildlife Refuge, North Carolina. A special "experimental population" provision of the Endangered Species Act was utilized for this landmark restoration project. The provision, adopted in 1982, provides greater flexibility for managing the habitat and populations of endangered species designated as experimental. The Fish and Wildlife Service has also used this designation for reestablished populations of various fishes, the Delmarva fox squirrel, and the sea otter. Efforts to reintroduce the Florida panther to unoccupied habitat are being initiated under the experimental population provision, as will future attempts to reintroduce gray wolves to regions where they are unlikely to return on their own—the greater Yellowstone ecosystem and the Southwest.

Cooperation with States

State and territory conservation agencies have a major role in the protection and recovery of resident threatened and endangered species. In recognition of this role, Section 6 of the Endangered Species Act provides for grant funding for work by states and U.S. territories with approved cooperative agreements. By November 1988 there were 51 cooperative agreements for animals and 36 agreements for plants. Three territories—Guam, Puerto Rico, and the Virgin Islands—have entered into cooperative agreements. The only states lacking agreements are Alabama and Louisiana.

The Reagan administration consistently attempted to eliminate Section 6 funding for state work on endangered species and thus to halt a program considered by many experts as the key to recovery for numerous species. Fortunately, the Congress refused to eliminate the funding for state work, but recent appropriations—$4.3 million in fiscal years 1987 and 1988—have been far from adequate. As a result of the funding uncertainty during the 1980s, the states have been reducing their requests for grants and curtailing their endangered species activities rather than expanding their efforts to accommodate the increasing number of listed species.

Nonetheless, a few species have benefited from Section 6 funding, including the California sea otter, grizzly bear, peregrine falcon, and some bird species native to Guam and Hawaii. Several states utilized portions of their Section 6 grants to fund surveys of freshwater mussels, and two states produced handbooks on endangered plants.

Making Recovery Plans Work

The Endangered Species Act mandates the development and implementation of recovery plans for all listed species unless the Secretary of the Interior or Commerce finds that a plan would not promote conservation of the species. Despite this requirement and the growing number of listed species, development and approval of new recovery plans have declined steadily since 1984. In 1987, only 15 new plans were approved by the Fish and Wildlife Service. The National Marine Fisheries Service did not approve any new plans. By September 30, 1988, the end of the fiscal year, 17 new additions brought the total number of approved recovery plans to 239. This means that just more than half—52 percent—of the listed U.S. species (276 of 528) were covered by approved plans (U.S. Fish and Wildlife Service 1988a).

Developing and approving recovery plans are only the first steps. To prevent extinctions and to effect recovery, the plans must be implemented. Experience indicates that only a small number of high priority species have benefited from active implementation of plans, while plans for other species languish on the shelf because of controversy, lack of funding, or low agency priority. Although difficult to document for recent years, it appears that less than half of the approved recovery plans are being implemented. Unfortunately, after 1984, the Fish and Wildife Service dropped its recovery plan implementation report and failed to initiate a much needed automated recovery tracking system. These actions, combined with the shift of primary responsibility for plan development and implementation to the regional offices, have made it virtually impossible to evaluate recovery program progress except on a plan-by-plan basis through the regional offices.

In 1988, the administration maintained that the urgency to develop and implement recovery plans was reduced because conflicts had been alleviated through the consultation process (see next section) and actions initiated by other federal agencies in compliance with their obligation under the Endangered Species Act to conserve listed species (U.S. Fish and Wildlife Service 1988b). Yet, in general, the service was not able to document this assertion. While this may have been the case in particular instances, the decline in recovery plan approval was widely attributed within the Fish and Wildlife Service and by conservationists to lowered priority and inadequate funding for endangered species work. For example, a coalition of conservation groups advocated appropriations of more than $12.2 million for recovery efforts in fiscal year 1988, but the administration requested only $5.8 million and the Congress finally appropriated $7.5 million (see table 2).

The continuing degradation of habitats, the decline and even extinction of listed species, and the increasing need for captive-breeding efforts to save and restore species demonstrate the urgent need to accelerate the development and implementation of recovery plans. The Congress agrees and has adopted an amendment to improve the recovery process.

Section 7 Consultations

Section 7 of the Endangered Species Act requires affirmative action by each federal agency to aid species and contains a mechanism to avoid or reduce conflicts between threatened and endangered species and government activities. All federal agencies are required to consult with the Fish and Wildlife Service or the National Marine Fisheries Service, as appropriate, to ensure that their actions will not jeopardize the existence of any listed species in the United States or abroad and will not destroy or adversely modify the species' critical habitat. The critical habitat provision currently affects only 103 listed species in the United States because such habitat has not been designated for the remaining 425 U.S. species or for any listed species in other countries.

Short, informal consultations suffice when it appears that potential conflicts can be resolved in favor of the species early in a project's planning. Whenever a proposed action "may affect" a listed species, a formal consultation and the preparation of a written biological opinion are required. These Fish and Wildlife Service opinions conclude either that the project is or is not likely to jeopardize a species' continued existence. If the service issues a "jeopardy" opinion, it must identify the "reasonable and prudent alternatives" that would avoid adverse impacts to the species. If no alternative is acceptable to project proponents, they may petition

Table 2. U.S. Fish and Wildlife Service Endangered Species Program Appropriations (in Millions of Dollars), Fiscal Years 1974-1988.

FY	1974	75	76	77	78	79	80
Total	4.657	5.542	9.486	13.330	16.534	18.869	20.087

FY	1981	82	83	84	85	86	87	FY 1988 Administration Request	Appropriated	Recommended by ESARC[1]
Total	22.782	17.769	20.459	22.205	26.944	28.824	29.764	23.670	31.066	53.723
Listing	4.101	1.987	2.057	2.595	3.191	3.071	3.622	3.222	3.259	7.0
Consultation	2.578	2.459	2.541	2.575	2.845	2.625	3.193	3.022	2.971	4.0
Permits	—	—	—	—	.718	.815	.866	.859	.855	.960
Recovery	4.629	5.217	5.129	4.714	5.884	6.031	6.565	5.819	7.512	12.2
Section 6	3.920	0	2.000	2.000	3.92	4.204	4.3	0	4.3	15.0
Research & Development	2.084	2.434	2.966	4.135	4.404	4.544	4.827	4.742	5.201	5.0
Law Enforcement	5.470	5.672	5.766	6.186	5.815	7.381	6.228	5.843	6.805	9.4
Fisheries, Hatchery Operations–ESA	—	—	—	—	.167	.153	.163	.163	.163	.163

[1]Endangered Species Act Reauthorization Coalition.

for an exemption by a special high-level committee with authority to decide whether the regional or national significance of a project outweighs the potential extinction of a particular species.

The Fish and Wildife Service may also allow the "incidental taking" of members of listed species through the consultation process or by special permit to private parties. The conditions and mitigating measures necessary to minimize adverse impacts to the species must be specified.

The number of consultations—13,824 in fiscal year 1987—has more than quadrupled since 1980. Of the total consultations, only 484 were formal and only 36 of those resulted in jeopardy opinions. Because consultation is mandated by the Endangered Species Act and affects other federal agencies, industry, and development projects, the Fish and Wildlife Service must commit whatever resources are necessary to meet the demand, often diverting those resources from species recovery work. The dramatic decline in new recovery plan approval since 1984 and the slow progress in plan implementation noted above are due in part to the combined effect of the consultation workload and the generally inadequate resources available for endangered species work.

In addition, under the Reagan administration the Fish and Wildlife Service did not establish a method of enforcing completion of the mitigating measures for incidental taking, nor has the agency put in place a consistent process for tracking the cumulative impacts on listed species of the actions it allows. The recovery of threatened and endangered species may have been further jeopardized as a result of these omissions and because political considerations sometimes outweigh biological ones in determining whether or not to issue a jeopardy opinion. For example, in a 1986 case involving Stacy Dam at the confluence of the Concho and Colorado rivers in Texas, the service bowed to pressures from the Texas congressional delegation and accepted mitigation measures it had previously rejected for the Concho water snake. Despite a lack of new data, the agency issued a second biological opinion and accepted a mitigation plan to create artificial habitat for the snake.

In 1981, Secretary of the Interior James Watt simply halted consultations on U.S. government projects overseas. When regulations to implement the congressional changes of 1979 and 1982 in Section 7 of the Endangered Species Act finally were published in 1986, the administration formally adopted abandonment of the consultation process for species outside the United States. Defenders of Wildlife, Friends of Animals and Their Environment, and the Humane Society of the United States challenged the new regulations in court (Fitzgerald 1988). The case is pending as of this writing.

Congressional committees also responded, first by recommending consultations for agency actions that might affect listed foreign species (in 1987 House Interior and Foreign Operations appropriations committee reports) and subsequently by declaring, "to the extent that these regulations attempt to restrict that each federal agency consult with the Secretary to ensure that its actions are not likely to jeopardize the continued existence and recovery of any listed species, the regulations have no statutory basis, are contrary to congressional intent and are contrary to law" (U.S. Congress, Senate Committee on the Environment and Public Works 1987). Introducing the Endangered Species Act reauthorization bill for floor consideration, Senator John Chafee of Rhode Island reaffirmed that the existing act requires "such consultations concerning listed species overseas" (U.S. Congress, Senate 1988).

Other Federal Agencies

How the Interior Department's Bureau of Land Management (BLM) and the Agriculture Department's Forest Service manage their multiple-use lands is of vital importance to the conservation of threatened and endangered species. Public lands administered by the BLM provide habitat for approximately 140 listed species and many hundreds of species awaiting listing. The National Forest System also provides vital habitat for numerous species awaiting listing and for approximately 150 listed species, including the grizzly bear, woodland caribou, red-cockaded woodpecker, and gray wolf.

Both agencies inventory habitats and participate in the development and implementation of recovery plans. In addition, habitat management plans or programs to prevent endangerment may be developed for selected candidate species or other species considered "sensitive." An unfortunate reality, however, is that these multiple-use land management agencies come under great pressure from timbering, grazing, mineral development, mining, and other interests to compromise protection of endangered and threatened plants and animals even though the law puts endangered species first.

The continuing and dramatic decline of both listed and unlisted desert tortoise populations on BLM lands, controversy over management of their habitats, and petitions to list all unlisted populations have prompted the BLM to develop a range-wide management plan. The objective of the plan is to restore grasses and other plants on which the tortoise depends by reducing livestock grazing levels, primarily by cattle.

But if the BLM is to actively contribute to the recovery of species on the lands that it manages, as the Endangered Species Act requires, its program budget must be enhanced and expert personnel added for recovery work. The bureau has no invertebrate biologists and too few fisheries biologists and botanists. Most BLM efforts are directed at basic species protection and survival rather than at recovery.

It is national forest land in the Southeast that many species such as the red-cockaded woodpecker depend on for survival, particularly mature pine forests with open understories. This woodpecker continues to decline because of habitat loss or degradation, although the Forest Service is adopting a more progressive and comprehensive view of species conservation. Nonetheless, the Forest Service has been unable so far—primarily because of inadequate resources and political will—to implement recovery plans except for a small number of high-priority species such as the grizzly bear in the Northern Rockies.

Unlike the BLM and the Forest Service, the National Park Service is not required to manage its lands for multiple uses, but rather to preserve the natural ecosystems as much as possible and maintain its lands for the enjoyment of the public. Thus, the Park Service has a unique opportunity and responsibility in the preservation and restoration of biological diversity. It plays a prominent role in the recovery of threatened and endangered species, including the peregrine falcon, grizzly bear, Rocky

The loss of our lands and waters to exploitation by humans has taken a great toll on the habitat of endangered wildlife, including fish, invertebrates, and plants.

Mountain wolf, Florida panther, and sea turtles.

But because the range and habitat of these and many other species are not restricted to the relatively protected lands of the National Park System, their continued survival and eventual recovery depend upon agency leadership and effective regional interagency cooperation and coordination.

Wildlife Habitat Acquisition

The loss of our lands and waters to exploitation by humans has taken a great toll on the habitat of endangered wildlife, including fish, invertebrates, and plants. Urban and rural development consumes 750,000 acres of forest and farmland each year in the United States alone and far more in the developing world. This nation alone has lost 450,000 acres of wetlands annually for more than 20 years. To reduce this loss of habitat, Section 5 of the Endangered Species Act requires a wildlife conservation plan and authorizes the acquisition of land essential to endangered, threatened, and other species through the Land and Water Conservation Fund Act and several other laws containing land acquisition provisions.

The Land and Water Conservation Fund is particularly important because it authorizes Congress to appropriate up to $900 million annually to purchase lands for national wildlife refuges, national parks, national forests, and the Bureau of Land Management as well as state lands for recreation and wildlife programs. In theory, the fund obtains its money from outer continental shelf oil and gas leases and royalties, surplus property sales, and motorboat fuel taxes—although these have actually been devoted to general revenue and not put into a designated trust fund.

The need to purchase more land is clear. Only approximately 70 of the hundreds of threatened and endangered species in the United States are believed to be protected on national wildlife refuges. Yet the Reagan administration generally opposed the appropriation of any funds from the Land and Water Conservation Fund to acquire land for refuges and supported very little funding for other national land conservation systems. Fortunately, the Congress has nevertheless provided substantial sums for wildlife habitat acquisition. Although appropriations from the fund were less than $200 million a year in fiscal year 1986, and 1987, and 1988, the Congress has supported the need to protect endangered species habitat. Allocations for refuge land acquisition for endangered species have increased, and other federal agencies have acquired some important land that benefits candidate or endangered species.

In fiscal year 1988, the administration requested funding only for refuge acquisition management and none for land purchases. The Congress appropriated nearly $49.9 million from the Land and Water Conservation Fund for refuge land acquisition, of which $39.9 million was for endangered species habitat. This money included the first funding for California's Sacramento River National Wildlife Refuge, which provides habitat for federal and state listed and candidate species. The

Congress targeted $4 million of the total to expand the range of the red wolf on Alligator River National Wildlife Refuge in North Carolina. In addition to the refuge funding, the Congress provided $600,000 to the Bureau of Land Management for desert tortoise habitat in the Mojave and Sonoran deserts of California.

Although for fiscal year 1989 the administration again requested funds only for refuge acquisition management, the Congress appropriated $52.7 from the Land and Water Conservation Fund for refuge land acquisition, with $41.9 million directed to buy habitat that specifically benefits endangered species. The BLM received more than $2 million in appropriations to secure more desert tortoise habitat in California.

Endangered species may also benefit from acquisition of wetlands. The Land and Water Conservation Fund provided more than $6.5 million to purchase part of the Pinhook Swamp for inclusion in the Osceola National Forest—acquiring some of the land needed to provide a habitat corridor linking that forest and the Okefenokee National Wildlife Refuge (see Harris article). This wildlife movement corridor will benefit many species, including the Florida panther proposed for reintroduction to the area.

The Congress ensured that funding for major land acquisition will continue by passing legislation in 1987 to extend the life of the Land and Water Conservation Fund for 25 years—until the year 2015.

Reauthorizing the Endangered Species Act: A Lesson in Perseverance

The Endangered Species Act of 1973 has been amended several times, most recently in 1988 at the close of the 100th Congress.

Long-term authority for funding to implement and enforce the act expired in 1985 and was not renewed until 1988. In the interim, the Congress provided funding on an annual basis.

Organized action for reauthorization began in early 1985, when the Endangered Species Act Reauthorization Coalition—a group of more than thirty scientific, animal welfare, and conservation organizations including Defenders of Wildlife—urged Congress to make the act more effective by

strengthening some of its provisions. The stage was set for lengthy debate when other interests urged Congress to weaken provisions and adopt additional exemptions to the law.

A modest reauthorization bill acceptable to the conservation coalition was approved by the House of Representatives but stalled in the Senate at the end of the 99th Congress in 1986. Led by Gerry Studds of Massachusetts, the House passed stronger legislation (H.R. 1467) in 1987 while rebuffing several attempts to delist individual species and otherwise weaken the act. On the Senate side, however, the legislation (S. 675) was mired by several senators seeking to weaken or stall implementation of the Endangered Species Act's protective provisions.

Senator George Mitchell of Maine, the bill's primary sponsor, and Senate majority leader Robert Byrd of West Virginia undertook determined efforts to work out disagreements as the 1988 elections approached and the conservation coalition stepped up its lobbying and media efforts. The long battle finally ended on October 7, 1988, when President Reagan signed into law amendments strengthening the Endangered Species Act and authorizing substantially increased levels of funding through fiscal year 1992.

The protection of sea turtles and the management of threatened predators (particularly the grizzly bear and the gray wolf) proved to be the most controversial issues during the 1987-88 congressional consideration of the act (Fitzgerald 1988).

Debate over the sea turtle centered on a 1987 regulation issued by the National Marine Fisheries Service that required shrimp trawlers in the Atlantic off the southeastern states and in the Gulf of Mexico to install turtle excluder devices (TEDs) to reduce turtle mortality from trawl nets. TEDs are mesh panels or grates that shunt sea turtles and other large objects out of the nets while allowing shrimp to enter and be caught. Each trawler may need up to four TEDs at a cost of about $40 to $400 each, depending on the design. The regulation followed years of discussion and negotiation based upon mounting evidence that trawl nets drown sea turtles of five threatened or endangered species. Rather than comply with the regulation, some shrimpers turned to their congressional representatives for relief.

In light of a perceived need for more testing in certain inshore waters (e.g., estuaries, bays, and barrier island channels) and a somewhat lesser risk to turtles associated with shorter inshore trawls, the House adopted a compromise that delayed the inshore regulations for two years. The battle raged on in the Senate, however, holding up the Endangered Species Act reauthorization for months. Ultimately, Senator Howell Heflin of Alabama dropped his threat to filibuster the bill when the Senate agreed to a further compromise, later accepted by the House in conference. The outcome: The regulation requiring TEDS does not go into

T he protection of sea turtles and the management of threatened predators (particularly the grizzly bear and the gray wolf) proved to be the most controversial issues during the 1987-88 congressional consideration of the Endangered Species Act.

effect for offshore areas until May 1, 1989, and for inshore areas until May 1, 1990. In addition, an independent study of sea turtle conservation is to be conducted by the National Academy of Sciences. If the Secretary of Commerce "determines that other conservation measures are proving equally effective in reducing sea turtle mortality by shrimp trawling," he is to modify the regulations for inshore areas accordingly (U.S. Congress, Senate 1988).

The grizzly bear and the wolf were the other major subjects of attempts to weaken protections for species. As noted earlier, the Endangered Species Act generally prohibits the taking of endangered species and directs the Secretary of the Interior to promulgate regulations for the conservation of threatened species. The specific requirements of the Act have been further interpreted by the courts. In *Sierra Club v. Clark*, the U.S. Court of Appeals for the 8th Circuit disallowed a sport trapping season on Minnesota's threatened timber wolf population proposed by the state and the Fish and Wildlife Service in 1982. The court found that the definition of conservation in the Endangered Species Act limits the use of regulated taking— sport hunting or trapping—to "the extraordinary case where population pressures within a given ecosystem cannot be otherwise relieved as stated in Section 3(3) of the Act" (*Sierra Club v. Clark* 1985).

1988 Amendments to the Endangered Species Act

The 100th Congress adopted a number of amendments strengthening the Endangered Species Act of 1973 and directing the government agencies responsible for implementing the act's provisions to take further action to conserve species in danger.

The amendments specify that the Fish and Wildlife Service and the National Marine Fisheries Service must:

• Monitor the status of all candidate species that have been found to qualify for listing but are awaiting action.

• List, on an emergency basis, any of the qualifying candidate species facing a significant risk.

• Standardize recovery plans to include site-specific management needs, measurable recovery criteria, timetables, and cost estimates.

• Report (through the Secretary of the Interior) biennially to Congress on the status of efforts to develop and implement recovery plans and on the status of species with plans.

• Monitor for five years, in cooperation with the states, populations of species delisted as recovered to ensure their continued viability and relist species if necessary to prevent a significant risk to their well being.

The Congress also:

• Increased protection for endangered plants by declaring that destroying or damaging such plants on federal lands and violating state law or regulations on nonfederal lands also constitute violations of federal law. (Previously, only collecting endangered plants from federal lands constituted a violation of the act.)

• Increased from $39 million in fiscal year 1985 to $66 million in fiscal year 1992 the level of appropriations authorized for activities undertaken by the federal agencies administering the act.

• Established for cooperative work with the states a "cooperative endangered species fund" to receive deposits not taken from but equal to five percent of the $300 million for game species in the Pittman-Robertson Wildlife Restoration Fund and the Dingell-Johnson Sport Fishing Restoration Account. However, these funds must still be appropriated by the Congress.

• Increased fines for violations of the act by 250 percent and provided that, after reserving $500,000 for rewards, the balance of the fund from all fines collected under the act is to be deposited in the cooperative endangered species conservation fund for state efforts.

• Adopted the African Elephant Conservation Act as an amendment to the Endangered Species Act, providing greater control over international trade in ivory and funds to help protect drastically declining African elephant populations.

Some state fish and wildlife agencies—like Montana's, fearing for its hunt on threatened grizzly bears, and others wanting to control wolves with fewer restrictions—prevailed upon the International Association of Fish and Wildlife Agencies to seek an amendment essentially overturning *Sierra Club v. Clark*. The issue was addressed at length and delayed the reauthorization bill in the Senate, although the amendment was never offered because of insufficient support. In the 100th Congress, the Senate Committee on the Environment and Public Works noted in its report on the reauthorization bill that no evidence had been presented to indicate that the Montana grizzly bear hunt did not fall within the extraordinary case exception to the general rule affirmed in *Sierra Club*

v. Clark (U.S. Congress, Senate 1987). The committee also reiterated the flexibility available in managing species when they are reintroduced under the experimental population provision of the act, as is proposed for restoring the gray wolf to Yellowstone National Park under the Northern Rocky Mountain Wolf Recovery Plan.

A New Opportunity

Fifteen years have passed since the Congress enacted the Endangered Species Act of 1973—realistically too little time to have saved the majority of our endangered and threatened species but more than enough time in which to have established an effective federal-state program to protect and recover species. It is clear, however, that the magnitude of the biological deficit we are facing looms as large as our nation's financial debt—and scientists warn that the biological deficit is of far greater consequence.

The actions of the Reagan administration throughout most of the 1980s exacerbated this critical problem. Valuable time and opportunities have been lost. Habitat and species that potentially could have been saved have been lost as well. Thousands of species are backlogged awaiting attention, while too little has been done for the

majority of "protected" animals and plants.

The Congress provided the legislative framework for action in 1973. In the 1988 reauthorization of the Endangered Species Act, the 100th Congress not only reaffirmed its intent to protect and recover endangered species but also refined and strengthened the framework for administrative action and approved funding levels for more aggressive agency implementation. The Congress specifically recognized the plight of the candidate species backlogged for listing and directed agency action to prevent further extinctions of these plants

Recommendations for Fully Implementing the Act

Defenders of Wildlife urges the Bush Administration to:

• Declare—preferably by executive order within the first months of 1989—that the maintenance of natural diversity, including the protection and recovery of endangered species, is the first priority of the nation's wildlife policy.

• Direct every federal agency to:

—designate an officer responsible for that agency's compliance with the Endangered Species Act;

—carry out "programs for the conservation of endangered species and threatened species" as required by Section 7(a)(1) of the act; and

—consult with the Secretary of the Interior or the Secretary of Commerce (through the Fish and Wildlife Service or National Marine Fisheries Service) as appropriate to ensure that all federal agency actions will jeopardize neither the continued survival nor the recovery of foreign or domestic species, as directed by the Congress.

• Request appropriations in fiscal year 1990 and subsequent years sufficient to:

—fully implement the act through the Fish and Wildlife Service, National Marine Fisheries Service, Bureau of Land Management, Forest Service, National Park Service, Animal and Plant Health Inspection Service, and other agencies;

—encourage and fully fund authorized and cooperative work with states and territories; and

—meet U.S. financial obligations under the Convention on International Trade in Endangered Species (CITES) and the Western Hemisphere Convention.

• Direct the Secretary of the Interior and the Secretary of Commerce to:

—complete the review of all Department of the Interior programs required in Section 7(a)(1) before fiscal year 1990 and concurrent review of other agency programs six months later (draft reviews should be published for

public comment by July 1 and December 1, 1989, respectively);

—develop or revise recovery plans for all listed species, unless findings conclusively show a particular species would not benefit from such a plan, giving priority to U.S. species and to foreign species (in cooperation with host countries whenever possible) that face significant and immediate threats to their survival;

—address the needs of multiple species in a single plan whenever feasible;

—make demonstrable progress in the implementation of all approved recovery plans and establish a system for tracking the status of listed species and the implementation of recovery plan tasks;

—evaluate and revise as appropriate the allocation of Section 6 grant funds to states to maximize benefits in the protection or restoration of the natural diversity of wildlife;

—monitor candidate species

and animals. The Congress also sought to remedy the shortcomings in recovery plans, and, by imposing a reporting requirement, to hold the agencies accountable for their progress in developing and implementing recovery plans as well as for the status of species with plans.

Last but not least, in establishing the cooperative endangered species fund, the Congress recognized that providing a sizable and steady source of funding for cooperative work with the states and territories to monitor candidate and recently recovered species as well as to benefit listed species is a vital step in a realistic nationwide program to protect and recover endangered and threatened species.

Thus, the nation has an opportunity to correct the mistakes of the past. With a revitalized law and a new administration, we have a new opportunity to build the program that can make a difference to future generations of Americans. We can either continue to squander our invaluable biological resources—the natural diversity of wild plants and animals—and endanger ourselves, or we can put the Endangered Species Act fully into effect.

---

awaiting listing decisions and promptly list species facing significant risks to their survival; define significant risk to include biological benchmarks that give rise to a "presumption of significant risk" and automatic emergency listing;

—prepare the first general wildlife conservation plan required by Section 5(a) of the act for public comment by the end of fiscal year 1989—with funding for its implementation in the fiscal year 1990 budget request—and implement the first plan in fiscal year 1990; and

—restore elements of the pre-1986 regulations concerning consultation to insure that the recovery of any species, domestic or foreign, is not jeopardized by any agency action, funding, or assistance and require more specific commitments and follow-up to insure that any incidental taking allowed does not impede recovery.

• Direct the Secretary of the Interior to:

—review the 1987 dismantling of the Office of Endangered Species and reestablish the office unless its intended roles in coordinating, oversight, and biological expertise are fully and specifically filled by other offices; and

—increase the annual listing rate and the efficiency and cost-effectiveness of the listing process by listing species in appropriate ecological or administrative groupings (e.g., county, state, habitat, community, ecosystem, or all of category one candidate species) whenever possible.

Defenders of Wildlife urges the 101st Congress to:

• Exercise close oversight of the implementation, including the development of new regulations, by the Bush administration of the Endangered Species Act as amended in 1988 and of the Convention on International Trade in Endangered Species.

• Appropriate authorized funding sufficient for full and aggressive implementation of the act, and for implementation of CITES, by all agencies with responsibility to implement it or to conduct programs to conserve endangered species.

• Pass legislation to establish the American Heritage Trust Fund, a dedicated trust from which up to $1 billion can be provided annually to purchase habitat, particularly critical linkages or corridors, for endangered and threatened wildlife, including fish and plants, and to promote biological diversity.

• Pass legislation improving and funding the Fish and Wildlife Conservation Act of 1980 (see Manville article) in order to preserve biological diversity and prevent endangerment by halting the decline of species and their habitats through cooperative efforts of state, federal, and private agencies toward better wildlife, water, and land management.

• Pass legislation to conserve biological diversity that, among other things, establishes an early warning system including assessments and biological presumptions of decreased diversity or significantly decreased viability of species or of ecosystems.

Ginger Merchant Meese served on the staff of Defenders of Wildlife specializing in endangered species from 1976 through 1988. Her work has encompassed a broad range of wildlife conservation issues from public land management and international treaty negotiation to the landmark reintroduction of the red wolf in the Southeast. She has been a principal author of Defenders' annual endangered species report since its inception in 1984. Ms. Meese earned her M.A. degree in physical anthropology from American University. She is now serving as executive vice-president of the National Wildlife Refuge Association.

The author recognizes the special contributions of John Fitzgerald, Defenders' counsel for wildlife policy, to this article—in particular, the sections on the 1988 reauthorization of the Endangered Species Act and recommendations for implementation.

Defenders of Wildlife gratefully acknowledges the help of Michael Bean, chairman of the Environmental Defense Fund's wildlife program and author of The Evolution of National Wildlife Law, *in reviewing and commenting on the manuscript.*

Selected Bibliography

Fitzgerald, J. M. 1988. Withering wildlife: Whither the Endangered Species Act? A review of amendments to the act. *Endangered Species Update* 5 (August): 27-34.

Sierra Club v. Clark. 1985. 755 F.2d 1506 (8th Circuit).

U.S. Congress. Senate Committee on the Environment and Public Works. 1987. Report No. 240. 100th Congress, 1st. Session. Washington, D.C.

U.S. Congress. Senate. 1988. Endangered Species Act Authorization. 100th Congress, 2nd Session. *Congressional Record.* Vol. 134. Daily ed. (25 July): S 9752-74.

U.S. Fish and Wildlife Service. 1987a. *Endangered Species Technical Bulletin* 12 (9): 4.

_____. 1987b. *Endangered Species Technical Bulletin* 12 (11-12): 1, 11.

_____. 1988a. Box score of U.S. list of threatened and endangered species and recovery plans, as of 30-Sep-88. *Endangered Species Technical Bulletin* 13 (3): 8.

_____. 1988b. 1989 fiscal year highlights: The Interior budget in brief—Fish and Wildlife Service. U.S. Department of the Interior, Washington, D.C.

U.S. Office of the Federal Register. 1988. *Federal Register* 53 (August 31): 335126.

A Funding Dilemma

By Albert M. Manville II

The Fish and Wildlife Conservation Act

Most Americans are aware that numerous species of wild animals and plants are on the brink of extinction because of human actions, primarily the destruction of habitat. More than 500 species in the United States alone are now officially listed under the Endangered Species Act as endangered or threatened with extinction.

But many people are not aware that *most* of our nation's native animal species and many plants are in a state of decline due to habitat degradation or loss. While it is the federal government that has responsibility for federally listed threatened and endangered species and migratory species, it is the states that bear responsibility for most of their resident wildlife. As described in the following article by Sara Vickerman, state fish and wildlife agencies have generally emphasized management programs for game animals desired by hunters and fishermen. Traditionally, the agencies have had neither the funds nor, in many cases, the inclination, to safeguard the health and abundance of all wildlife in their states.

The Congress passed the Fish and Wildlife Conservation Act in 1980 to aid efforts aimed at halting the decline of species. Popularly referred to as the "Nongame Act," the legislation deals with wild animals that are not hunted, fished, or trapped. Those fauna comprise about 90 percent of our indigenous vertebrate wildlife, including 350 species of mammals, 654 species of birds, 470 species of amphibians and reptiles, and 630 species of fish. The many thousands of invertebrate species are not now covered by the act.

The Fish and Wildlife Conservation Act is intended to do for nongame programs what the Pittman-Robertson Federal Aid in Wildlife Restoration Act and the Dingell-Johnson Federal Aid in Sport Fish Restoration Act have done for game management programs. Those two federal aid acts place excise taxes on hunting and fishing equipment, respectively—with receipts used primarily to benefit game species through habitat restoration, fish and wildlife research, and education. The Pittman-Robertson and Dingell-Johnson programs serve as direct public funding mechanisms for wildlife conservation activities, without requiring appropriations from the federal budget. The Fish and Wildlife Conservation Act is meant to provide funds for more comprehensive programs to help protect nongame wildlife through matching grants to the states. Unfortunately, since the act was adopted, the executive branch has requested not one penny for the state grants program, nor has the Congress appropriated any funds.

The need for full funding and implementation of the Fish and Wildlife Conservation Act has never been greater. Since the act was adopted nearly a decade ago, some 100 vertebrate species native to the United States have been added to the endangered species list. Hundreds more are candidates for listing, and the status of many more is yet to be determined. In addition, at least 30 species of nongame migratory birds are in peril (U.S. Fish and Wildlife Service 1987a). These, too, could become candidates for listing unless quick action is taken to protect them and their habitats. Comprehensive wildlife conservation efforts are urgently needed to prevent the endangerment of more and more species.

What the Act Does

As originally passed in 1980 and as reauthorized by Congress in 1986 and 1988, the Fish and Wildlife Conservation Act sets an annual appropriations ceiling of $5 million. It also envisions the development of additional sources of funds. But whether funds are appropriated, redirected, or accrued through off-budget means, the money is to be used for a matching grant program—three federal dollars for every state dollar—to reimburse states for development and implementation of nongame conservation plans. Under these plans, state fish and wildlife agencies are to evaluate the status of nongame species, identify critical habitats, and ultimately find the most cost-effective means for protecting the habitat and preventing the decline of nongame wildlife.

The act requires the Secretary of the Interior to advise Congress of potential off-budget (nonappropriated) funding sources that could be used for implementation. In 1985, an Interior Department report to the Congress listed 18 major potential sources of funding along with a number of supplemental possibilities (U.S. Fish and Wildlife Service 1985). However, at the request of the Office of Management and Budget, the report failed to recommend which sources would be the most equitable, reliable, innovative, and substantial or which

> *The need for full funding and implementation of the Fish and Wildlife Conservation Act has never been greater.*

might work best in a funding package. Since the release of the report, several additional potential mechanisms have been suggested.

Matching State Nongame Funds

A number of states have developed innovative programs to generate funds in order to meet the state share of the anticipated matching grants. Most notable is the state income tax check-off instituted by Colorado in 1977 and adopted after 1980 by many other states. Check-offs were initially quite successful, but because of problems including increased competition from check-offs added for other purposes, net income has been declining in some states (Inkley et al. 1988). Vickerman's article includes an analysis and summary table of the current status of check-off revenues in all fifty states. The long-term success of the check-off program is uncertain, with few states experiencing the steady growth of revenues that was initially expected.

The funding situation for nongame programs has, for the most part, worsened. Although state fish and wildlife agencies are trying hard to bring in more funds, they are not able to implement the comprehensive nongame programs needed without federal assistance. It is important to note that state funding mechanisms were intended to complement the federal matching grants, not to replace federal funding. Appropriation of the Fish and Wildlife Conservations Act's authorized $5 million would be a show of good faith to states that have been waiting since 1980 for matching grants. These funds could serve as seed money until an off-budget funding mechanism such as an earmarked excise tax is developed and implemented. But efforts by conservationists to get funds appropriated so far have been unsuccessful.

A coalition of conservation groups including Defenders of Wildlife has attempted over the last few years to come to agreement on strategy, direction, funding, and ultimate implementation of the Fish and Wildlife Conservation Act. Unfortunately, these groups have essentially approached the issues from their separate viewpoints rather than coming together with a single environmental voice. Some members of Congress and others have become frustrated at the apparent inability of conservationists to work together on this issue. The message from the Congress now seems clear: The conservation community has one last chance to support and lobby for a funding mechanism in the 101st Congress. Otherwise, the act may not even be reauthorized.

A Growing Constituency

Perhaps the greatest potential source of support for funding the act is the wildlife-watching American public—so far essentially silent on this issue. Nongame wildlife-related activities are of great interest to Americans. A 1980 survey by the Fish and Wildlife Service and the Bureau of the Census found that 83 million adults engaged in watching, photographing, or feeding birds or other wildlife in 1980, and 93 million participated in some form of nonconsumptive wildlife activity that year (U.S. Fish and Wildlife Service 1982). By 1985, when the national survey of fishing, hunting, and wildlife-associated recreation was conducted again, this constituency had expanded dramatically: 110 million Americans (more than half of all adults) actively participated in nonconsumptive wildlife-related activities, and 74 percent were classified as "nonconsumptive participants" (U.S. Fish and Wildlife Service 1987b). These numbers continue to grow. Birdwatching, in fact, is currently ranked as one of this country's most popular outdoor recreational activities.

Although the wildlife-viewing constituency is not particularly vocal or well organized, it represents the great majority of Americans, who enjoy wildlife in nonconsumptive ways and who believe it is the responsibility of the government to prevent species from being exterminated.

Potential Funding Mechanisms

Based on the needs of state nongame conservation efforts, Defenders of Wildlife in 1986 and again in 1988 recommended a package of funding options taken largely from the 1985 Interior Department report. These recommendations would not increase the federal deficit—and together have the potential to bring in at least $329 million annually. The package includes a $25 fee for mining claims on federal lands generating an estimated $30 million per year, a federal minerals severence tax projected to raise $120 million, a fee or tax for development of some federal lands generating at least $5 million per year, fees for other consumptive uses or services from federal lands supplying $100 million in new revenues, and excise taxes and semipostal stamps that could bring in $74-84 million. However, no action on these recommendations was taken by Congress.

The General Accounting Office (GAO) analyzed two potential funding mechanisms in 1988. One, redirecting the excise tax on fuels used in machinery such as lawn and garden equipment, appears to hold great promise (Duffus et al. 1988a). The tax is on fuel, not on the equipment, and its use for nongame wildlife conservation is both logical and appropriate. The tax would be redirected from non-highway-related use of machinery that can and often does negatively affect some wildlife species through habitat loss or degradation. The funds would also be significant (revenues ranging from $21-48 million per year) and stable, important requirements for an effective funding mechanism.

The second potential funding mechanism analyzed by the GAO is a voluntary semipostal stamp selling for more than the cost of regular first-class postage, estimated to produce surcharge revenues of perhaps $12 million per year (Duffus et al. 1988b). Many conservation organizations have not supported these or other voluntary funding mechanisms as sole-source options, believing that they will prove inadequate. However, if such voluntary mechanisms were used to supplement a more reliable permanent funding source, conservationists would be more likely to support them.

Other funding possibilities not analyzed in the GAO report include diverting funds attributable to the use of off-road vehicles from the Highway Trust Fund to the Fish and Wildlife Conservation Act. The same rationale as that for the redirected fuel tax on lawn and garden equipment applies.

There has also been some discussion about imposing user fees that would enable members of the public who participate in nonconsumptive wildlife recreation to help pay for wildlife conservation. These might include access fees to certain refuges and other public lands, excise taxes on products and equipment used in viewing and feeding wildlife, and related sources. In principle, Defenders of Wildlife and some other conservation organizations find user fees acceptable and support them as part of a package that would include general funding sources and mitigation funding (fees to cover the costs of damage to habitat from activities such as clearcutting and strip mining).

In the early 1980s, a proposal was made to impose an excise tax on wild bird seed, a large market to tap since birdseed sales in this country alone stood at more than $1 billion in 1987. The proposal failed in part because of concerns that the majority of those buying birdseed—the elderly and retirees on fixed incomes—would find the tax regressive and concerns that the tax might make it cost-prohibitive to buy birdseed. Opposition also came from the birdseed industry. Although the National Wildlife Federation tried to revive this option in 1988, the effort again failed.

Coordinating State and Federal Efforts for Wildlife Conservation

It is imperative that we bring endangered species back from the edge of extinction and that we protect viable populations of those species commonly classified as game species. These efforts alone, however, do not constitute effective wildlife conservation. We must start looking at all wildlife on an ecosystem basis if we are to halt the decline of our native species.

Under current law, the federal government has an obligation to conserve migratory birds, threatened and endangered species, and marine wildlife, as well as a shared obligation with the states to conserve other wildlife on federal lands. Section 5(a) of the Endangered Species Act requires the Secretary of the Interior to "establish and implement a program to conserve fish, wildlife, and plants," including but not limited to threatened and endangered species. These responsibilities should be fully carried out, and the criteria developed under the Fish and Wildlife Conservation Act for state wildlife management programs should be coordinated with existing federal efforts. Such co-

ordination would ensure attention to the need for identifying and protecting the most serious habitat gaps and providing for wildlife movement corridors, with the goal of preventing the endangerment of species and preserving biological diversity.

The immediate challenge before the conservation community and the Congress is to develop and approve a comprehensive funding package for the Fish and Wildlife Conservation Act. Time is running out for too many wildlife species.

Albert M. Manville II is the senior staff wildlife biologist for Defenders of Wildlife, leading the organization's marine entanglement and plastic pollution programs and efforts to strengthen federal nongame conservation activities. He received a Ph.D. degree in wildlife ecology and management from Michigan State University and holds his M.S. in natural resources/wildlife management and his B.S. in zoology. He has published articles on bear biology, nongame wildlife issues, marine entanglement, and general ecology.

Selected Bibliography

Duffus, J. III, B. Robinson, L. White, C. Kirby, E. Williams, and T. Goforth. 1988a. Resource protection: Using gasoline taxes to fund the Nongame Act. Report B-229454 (January 29). U.S. General Accounting Office, Washington, D.C.

_____. 1988b. Resource protection: Using semipostal stamps to fund the Nongame Act. Report B-229453 (February 1). U.S. General Accounting Office, Washington, D.C.

Inkley, D., A. Strong, L. Mills, and J. Feierabend. 1988. Funding state nongame programs: How much is enough? National Wildlife Federation, Washington, D.C.

U.S. Fish and Wildlife Service. 1982. National survey of fishing, hunting, and wildlife-associated recreation, 1980. U.S. Department of the Interior, Washington, D.C.

_____. 1985. Potential funding sources to implement the Fish and Wildlife Conservation Act of 1980. *Biological Report* 85 (5). U.S. Department of the Interior, Washington, D.C.

_____. 1987a. Migratory nongame birds of management concern in the United States: The 1987 list. U.S. Department of the Interior, Washington, D.C.

_____. 1987b. National survey of fishing, hunting, and wildlife-associated recreation, 1985. U.S. Department of the Interior, Washington, D.C.

State Wildlife Protection Efforts

By Sara E. Vickerman

The Nongame Programs

No discussion of the overall effort to protect wildlife communities would be complete without a special focus on nongame programs at the state and federal level. The term "nongame" refers to the vast majority of animals, and sometimes plants, not commonly taken for commercial or sport purposes.

Although the stated goals of nongame programs vary, it is generally acknowledged that, among government programs established to prevent the decline of native wildlife, the nongame programs are the ones most likely and appropriate to address the problem. But, while there has been tremendous growth and improvement in the programs over the past decade, most observers agree that the level of effort devoted to the goal of conserving the nation's diverse wildlife resources remains critically low in relation to the need.

Primary jurisdiction over nongame wildlife is shared by the federal government—which has management responsibility for migratory birds, marine mammals, and threatened and endangered species—and the states, which have responsibility for all wildlife not specifically under federal jurisdiction. However, the statutes really do not offer much coherent direction. Federal wildlife law, ac-

cording to one authority, "to the extent that it can be described as a body of law, remains fragmented among jurisdictions, incomplete, without a guiding rationale, and mostly unknown" (Coggins 1975). State wildlife law is even less cohesive, and the states create additional administrative distinctions among game, nongame, state-listed threatened and endangered, and completely unprotected wildlife species. In general, nongame and endangered species programs are combined at the state level and kept administratively separate at the federal level, adding to the overall confusion.

Accountability for preventing the decline of native wildlife species is difficult to establish given the fact that the various wildlife agencies sharing jurisdiction over the animals have control over very little of the habitat upon which the animals depend for survival. The agencies also have little regulatory authority beyond the establishment of open seasons and bag limits and the artificial propagation of individual species. Although some agencies, like the Forest Service, U.S. Department of Agriculture, have the statutory responsibility to conserve biological diversity, the specific actions needed to accomplish this goal are poorly defined, and the diversity requirement tends to conflict with commodity uses of the land. The result is that this responsibility often gets overlooked in the process of allocating resources.

Funding for Nongame Programs

The scattered responsibility for wildlife and habitat protection is not the only factor limiting effective conservation of the nation's wildlife heritage. Another serious obstacle was imposed inadvertently years ago, when wildlife management programs were initiated primarily for the purpose of meeting the demands of consumptive users for certain species such as deer, elk, and trout. Agencies grew to depend on consumptive user fees, and "he who pays the piper calls the tune" accurately describes the manner in which wildlife agency programs have been shaped by their funding source. Although a number of state wildlife programs and the federal programs are increasingly financed by general revenues, the level of appropriated funds is unlikely to meet the rapidly expanding need in the near future.

Since 1980, when Congress passed the Fish and Wildlife Conservation Act authorizing up to $5 million for state nongame management grants, agencies and conservationists have looked to the federal government for funding help. However, no funds have been appropriated under the authority of this act, and no other means of raising federal funds has ever been adopted. In fact, although the act was reauthorized for two more years in 1986, U.S. Fish and Wildlife Service opposition to its implementation and the apparent unwillingness of conservation groups to expend the necessary coordinated effort to encourage congressional action have hampered serious analysis of funding options.

In spite of this lack of federal encouragement, the number and size of the state nongame programs have increased gradually since 1980. Several states have developed very sophisticated programs, but generally their expansion has been limited by the factors affecting many government programs: efforts to reduce the federal deficit; cutbacks in grants to the states, such as Section 6 funds under the Endangered Species Act; declining oil revenues; weak farm economies; declining tax bases in agricultural areas; and proliferating check-off boxes in competition with the "nongame" check-off on some state tax forms. The result has been generally declining revenue for nongame wildlife programs.

Demographic Trends

In addition to these administrative and funding difficulties, most fish and wildlife agencies do not see the protection of entire native plant and animal communities as their primary goal. Although different constituencies make different demands on the agencies, attitude surveys tend to show strong support for the notion that the government should not allow any species to become extinct. This information suggests that a wide gap exists between agency priorities (often focused on single game species) and public expectations.

Fish and wildlife agencies have been reluctant to respond to other important social, economic, and demographic trends. For example, traditional income from the sale of hunting licenses is eroding, and there has been a corresponding decline in Pittman-Robertson Program funds derived from an 11 percent tax on hunting equipment. Meanwhile, although nonconsumptive wildlife recreation is increasing, few agencies recognize the potential for soliciting political and economic support from "nonconsumptive users." Other demographic trends suggest that interest in consumptive use (particularly hunting and trapping) may decline further as people move from rural to metropolitan areas and make the transition from an agricultural and manufacturing economy to more sedentary pursuits. This trend is certain to intensify pressure for a change in priorities (Naisbitt 1982).

As the states' nongame programs have been patched together over the last ten years or so, there has been no consistent interpretation as to where they fit within the traditional natural resource agency bureaucracies. Few states have acknowledged the level of effort—and amount of money— that will be required to prevent the extinction of native flora and fauna and to accommodate the growing demand for opportunities to view and photograph wildlife. Even fewer have planned accordingly. The federal government has failed to set the example and provide the proper incentive for the states to take this responsibility seriously. Meanwhile, many of the states seem to be waiting for Congress to finally fund the Fish and Wildlife Conservation Act.

State Nongame Program Surveys

Defenders of Wildlife conducted surveys and extensive interviews in 1986 and 1987 with conservationists in each state to find out how much has been accomplished in the last decade to protect wildlife communities and to determine what needs to be done next. A description and analysis of nongame and endangered species programs in the 50 states and at the federal level, based on the information obtained in these surveys and interviews, is provided below. The existing programs are described, highlighting the innovative approaches likely to set the stage for the growth and improvement of the overall effort in the 1990s.

This analysis is followed by recommendations of wildlife conservation goals and some specific suggestions for implementation directed towards the state and federal agencies bearing the primary responsibility for protecting our wildlife heritage.

Analysis of State Nongame and Endangered Species Programs

The information in this section, unless otherwise noted, was obtained through two mail surveys, extensive follow-up telephone interviews with the directors of nongame programs in each state, and discussions with other individuals knowledgeable about the programs. The fish and wildlife agency response rate was 100 percent in 1986 and 1987. In the second year, the survey was expanded to include natural heritage programs to provide a more accurate overview of state wildlife conservation efforts. Survey data are summarized state-by-state in the tables at the end of this article.

Program Goals

Determining the goals for any program is critical to its success. The survey revealed a tremendous variety in nongame wildlife program direction. Several states have no nongame program but do work on threatened and endangered species. Others focus on enhancing opportunities for people to enjoy wildlife. Some emphasize education. Most have a few high-visibility projects, usually involving eagles, peregrine falcons, or other popular species. Only a handful of state programs seem to be clearly focused on the goal of preventing the decline of all indigenous nongame wildlife species. The programs that are closely associated with natural heritage programs—established by The Nature Conservancy to inventory natural areas and certain rare plant and animal species—seem more likely to have a habitat protection approach.

Comprehensive Plans

The Fish and Wildlife Conservation Act requires state agencies to develop comprehensive wildlife plans in order to obtain federal grant funding when (and if) it becomes available. The act would allow states to use the funds to develop the plans. Our survey asked whether each agency had developed a comprehensive plan that would comply with the federal act requirements. Only 21 states responded affirmatively in 1987, although several others indicated that plans were being developed (see table 2). Generally, the existing plans reflect the meager funding allocated to nongame programs and seldom contain a viable strategy for building a new constituent base and securing new revenue sources.

Even when plans exist, converting them to actual work on the ground can be a challenge because of daily demands and endless crises. The result is a tendency for the programs to be reactive. Given limited resources and lack of enthusiastic administrative support, it is extremely difficult for nongame program biologists to develop and implement viable long-range plans.

Statutes and Regulations

Fish and wildlife agencies are governed by widely variable statutes and regulations. Most are confusing and contradictory, particularly to the extent that the legal definition of species and categories of organisms scatters management authority. According to our survey, only six states (Georgia, Hawaii, Massachusetts, Missouri, Texas, and Wisconsin) have consolidated responsibility for the protection of vertebrates, invertebrates, and plants under the same agency.

However, statutory authority generally is not the limiting factor in the establishment of effective programs to conserve wildlife. Most state and federal wildlife policies and laws direct the agencies to protect native wildlife and provide recreational opportunities for the public. Many statutes are broader than the programs established by the agencies, and most offer the wildlife department considerable discretion in the allocation of resources. The major weaknesses in state statutes concern the lack of authority of wildlife agencies to limit the destruction of significant habitats by private parties and other agencies.

Research

Most nongame personnel conduct some wildlife research and contract with universities or other professionals to investigate specific problems. However, the selection of projects often appears opportunistic or driven by individual interests rather than based on a coherent effort to channel funds into the most productive areas. Many of the small grants programs tend to fund a number of unsolicited requests instead of allocating funds according to a set of priorities in a plan.

In general, the traditional nongame program is primarily research oriented, and the most common subject of inquiry is a single species of wildlife, although no state has completed status surveys for most of its nongame species. Several states have relatively complete information on the federally listed threatened and endangered species, particularly those states in which a natural heritage program initiated the effort. Massachusetts and Washington have two of the most complete data bases, in which the nongame and endangered species programs are fully integrated with the natural heritage programs.

Although no state has completed a comprehensive habitat inventory, there have been some limited efforts to define and protect high priority wildlife habitats. For example, the Nevada Department of Wildlife conducted an inventory of the riparian habitat and wildlife species along the Humboldt River as the first step in a cooperative effort to influence land management practices in the area (Rawlings 1987). There have been some efforts to use satellite technology for systematic habitat inventories, but, in general, ecologically oriented research has been extremely limited.

Habitat acquisition is an essential component of any nongame wildlife conservation program. Yet only a few states have significant land acquisition programs.

The heavy emphasis on single species research may have contributed to the obscurity and isolation of the weaker programs. Unless the research is focused on a specific problem and results are widely published with management recommendations, the information may be lost in the files of the agency.

Habitat Conservation

Although habitat acquisition is an essential component of any nongame wildlife conservation program, only a few states (California, Florida, Hawaii, Illinois, Massachusetts, Minnesota, Missouri, South Carolina, and Washington) have significant land acquisition programs. Since 1984, there have been several successful state efforts to secure habitat acquisition funding through general obligation bonding. These measures, although not specifically focused on "nongame" habitat needs as defined by the fish and wildlife agency, have provided funding to buy areas important to wildlife in general and endangered species in particular.

In 1984, 64 percent of California voters approved an $85 million general obligation bond for the acquisition and protection of habitats, including wetlands and the habitats of threatened and endangered species. In 1988, a similar measure authorizing $776 million to purchase parks and coastal and wildlife areas was approved by California voters. New York voters recently approved a bond issue that includes $250 million for habitat acquisition. In Illinois, wildlife is one of the beneficiaries of the governor's "Build Illinois Program," in which $20 million was appropriated to be spent over five years at $4 million per year. The intent is to preserve the natural heritage of Illinois by direct acquisition of habitat. Several properties under consideration for 1986 and 1987 include a heronry, an eagle refuge, and sites with threatened and endangered species of animals and plants (Tetreault 1986). The "Reinvest in Minnesota Program" has been enormously successful in generating public support and funding through the sale of general obligation bonds. Other bonds were approved by Maine and Massachusetts voters, and a campaign was initiated in Georgia in 1988.

Florida has one of the most elaborate land acquisition programs, involving several agencies and millions of dollars annually. Many of the habitats already purchased or under consideration for purchase are important to nongame and endangered species. In several states, there is close cooperation between the nongame and natural heritage programs in identifying natural areas with high wildlife values.

However, the tendency for wildlife agencies to place a higher priority on lands suitable for waterfowl production, ungulate winter range, and upland bird habitat remains strong. To the extent that fish and wildlife agencies do focus on habitat, the activities are frequently manipulative in nature and intended to maximize the production of one or more species, generally for consumptive use. These goals can conflict with the objective of providing habitat for a diversity of wildlife and can at times adversely affect nongame and even endangered species. For example, one state wildlife agency acquired a swamp and then channeled a stream to flood the area for waterfowl. Others use specially designed boats to open wetlands by removing vegetation and creating new stream channels. In one case, agency modification of a wetland destroyed the world's only known population of a species of water beetle. Lampricides and other fish poisons used to promote desired game fish like salmon and trout sometimes kill rare fishes. One fish and game agency constructed a boat launch in a loon nesting area. The common practice of converting natural habitat to large agricultural fields to produce grain for game birds and to open the area for hunters can destroy nongame habitat. Introducing exotic wildlife and fish can also displace native species.

Environmental Assessments

The responsibility for responding to requests from other state and federal agencies for review of environmental assessments concerning land use decisions or development plans often falls on nongame divisions. Unfortunately, adequate resources to thoroughly review each proposal are seldom available, tending to keep wildlife managers just one step ahead of the bulldozers and generally in a reactive mode. Although there has been some discussion about requiring the agencies or industries proposing habitat destruction to pay for the ecological assessment rather than using scarce wildlife conservation dollars, there has not been a concerted effort to generate mitigation fees to protect wildlife communities.

Education

Several state nongame programs place a heavy emphasis on wildlife education. Alaska's nongame program expends nearly half of its budget on the preparation and distribution of materials to every school in the state. The materials are unique to Alaska and include lessons on a variety of current issues, such as the aerial hunting of wolves by the Alaska Department of Fish and Game. Georgia's program has produced films on alligators, woodpeckers, sea turtles, gopher tortoises, and indigo snakes. Alabama published several high-quality booklets on the state's endangered wildlife. Minnesota and Florida have developed attractive publications on landscaping for wildlife. Some nongame programs help finance "Project Wild" educational materials, which are distributed to the schools by wildlife agencies.

Utah has taken a unique approach, working directly with the universities to develop curricula with a nongame and habitat orientation useful to students who may become future staff members of the state's fish and wildlife agency.

Public Relations

Nongame programs present a special problem for government agencies. In most other areas, government agencies are not expected to raise private funds for their programs, which are tax-supported. But the need to raise nongame funds puts the agencies in a new "business" and requires particular attention to public relations work. Since most state nongame programs are dependent on contributions through income tax check-offs or other voluntary mechanisms, funding and program viability are related directly to the level of public awareness and acceptance. The advantage of this arrangement is that the agencies must be somewhat responsive to the public's concerns. The disadvantage is that effective public relations programs are expensive and dilute, sometimes significantly, the funds available for wildlife projects.

Few agencies do an effective job of promoting their nongame programs, for a variety of reasons: These programs may be a low priority with agency directors or commissions; the information and education section may not be helpful or adequately funded; and nongame staff usually do not have the expertise, time, or funds to manage a professional public relations campaign. The level of public awareness and support for wildlife programs varies considerably from state to state.

Several state fish and wildlife agencies have taken steps to improve their public images and increase support for nongame programs. For example, a survey of Kansas residents to determine their attitudes toward nongame wildlife found that, although less than two percent of the respondents contribute to the program through the tax check-off, 90.3 percent believe it is important to protect wildlife. The report concluded that check-off promotion efforts should target students, white collar workers, tax preparers, and urban residents (Broadway n.d.).

The Arizona Department of Game and Fish conducted a public attitude survey that focused on new funding mechanisms. The survey report noted: "Nonconsumptive enthusiasts are understandably wary of contributing to a 'game' agency. . . . The wildlife agency, therefore, needs to keep the public well informed and happy with regard to nongame programs in order to successfully bring in voluntary contributions" (Greenberg 1985). The report encouraged the department to "broaden [its] range of clientele to include the significant numbers of nonconsumptive wildlife enthusiasts" and to change its name to indicate the spectrum of services it provides.

Unfortunately, a number of public relations

Development of a well-informed and supportive constituency is essential if new funding sources are to be secured for state nongame programs.

efforts undertaken by the state agencies have produced undetermined benefits. Program managers sometimes assume that projects involving highly visible species like eagles will automatically attract public support and donations to the programs. Others have expended substantial sums of money on posters and other promotional materials that may not significantly increase contributions to the program.

During the last few years, a number of states have contracted with media consultants and advertising agencies to carefully target the audiences most likely to respond to a request for support. An analysis of check-off revenues in 1987 revealed that most of the states with increases in tax check-off contributions relied on outside firms to promote the program (Vickerman 1987).

Many states have citizen advisory committees to work with the agencies in implementing their nongame programs. When they were originally constituted, the committees were heavily technical and academic in orientation. More recently, advisory committees have been broadened to include members with political expertise and to represent specific constituent groups. Although some advisory committees are more effective than others, their productivity seems to be directly related to the level of support given the committee by the agency and the degree to which the committee's advice is utilized.

Several agencies have searched for a more appealing term to replace "nongame." For example, California has initiated a new "Natural History" program that encompasses the traditional nongame, endangered species, and nonconsumptive wildife recreation efforts. "Watchable Wildlife" is a term used to describe the public relations programs aimed at the viewing public. Wyoming has copyrighted "Wyoming's Wildlife—Worth the Watching" and developed a high visibility marketing program intended to generate economic benefits for the state's tourism industry.

In any case, an agency's commitment to the effective marketing of nongame programs is critical to the maintenance of revenue from voluntary funding mechanisms. In the long run, development of a well-informed and supportive constituency is essential if new funding sources are to be secured.

Wildlife Rehabilitation and Damage Control

As people and wildlife expand into each other's territory, conflicts are inevitable. Several nongame programs are actively involved in assisting the public (and wildlife) with such conflicts. For example, in Arizona, a wildlife rehabilitation project is operated in conjunction with the Game and Fish Department. A portion of Oregon's nongame funds pays for private rehabilitation efforts. Although expensive and time consuming, rehabilitation programs appeal to the public and, if operated by private organizations, take the burden away from the agencies.

Most nongame programs also offer advice to landowners concerning techniques to reduce wildlife damage to property and crops. Requests for such advice are likely to increase over time, and wildlife managers will be increasingly called upon to help prevent the destruction of wildlife by agricultural interests. However, there has been very little research on specific techniques to prevent damage to crops and minimize the adverse impact on wildlife, and not much effort has been devoted to the integration of new, nonlethal techniques into government damage control efforts.

Nonconsumptive Wildlife Recreation

Birdwatching, whale watching, photography, and other nonconsumptive wildlife recreation activities are growing at a phenomenal rate. In Oregon, for example, nonconsumptive wildlife recreation days increased from 7 million in 1976 to 27 million in 1986. A Kansas study found that 75.2 percent of the population enjoyed watching wildlife (Broadway n.d.). The 1987 national survey conducted by the U.S. Fish and Wildlife Service and Bureau of the Census documented an increase in the number of adult Americans participating in nonconsumptive wildlife recreation from 55 percent in 1980 to 74 percent in 1985. Most wildlife agencies now acknowledge this important trend and recognize the value of recruiting casual wildlife enthusiasts as a new constituency. However, they continue to struggle with the means by which the new groups may be taken into the fold.

One challenge is defining the nature of appreciative "use" of the wildlife resource in order to extract user fees from the wildlife watchers and photographers. California has initiated an elaborate plan to charge entrance fees on certain wildlife areas open to the viewing public. Texas is exploring an annual fee with related benefits including land access and educational materials.

There has been considerable discussion at the federal level of imposing excise taxes on birdseed, cameras, film, binoculars, and related products to establish a funding base similar to the successful Pittman-Robertson and Dingell-Johnson programs. The response, however, has not been enthusiastic from the consuming public or the industries subject to the proposed taxes.

When state nongame programs were first established, nonconsumptive use, to the extent that it was acknowledged at all, was a part of the nongame program. The terms were used almost interchangeably until recently. There is now a concerted effort, led by Oregon, Colorado, and other states, to separate the nongame and endangered species programs administratively from the "watchable wildlife" programs. The former are considered to be research and management, as a subset of the game programs, usually in wildlife divisions. Wildlife recreation is managed by public affairs divisions and places a heavy emphasis on information and education about viewing opportunities.

This arrangement seems at times to create competition between the watchable wildlife and nongame programs for attention and funding, although it offers some potential for fully integrating recreation, education, and conservation goals within a single agency.

In recent years, there has been increasing emphasis on the economic value of nonconsumptive wildlife recreation. A survey conducted by the U.S. Fish and Wildlife Service in 1985 found that Americans spent about $14 billion on primary nonconsumptive wildlife recreational pursuits. Birdseed sales doubled between 1980 and 1985 from about $500 million to more than $1 billion. Wyoming applied multipliers to the federal data and determined that $678 million is spent annually on wildlife observation in the state. Oregon's Tourism Division helped finance two projects initiated by Defenders of Wildlife—a wildlife viewing guide and a study of the economic impact of nonconsumptive wildlife recreation. The tourism department of British Columbia hired a consulting firm to prepare a report on the economic potential of wildlife viewing in the province. The overall assessment is that the already substantial economic impact will be much greater when the opportunities for nonconsumptive uses are developed and promoted.

Structure, Management, and Staff of Nongame Wildlife Programs

Often when new programs are initiated, the old structures do not readily accommodate them. The placement and structure of state nongame and endangered species programs seem to be constantly changing, as if no one is quite sure what to do with them. Most states combine endangered species and nongame programs, sometimes because the same person is responsible for both. Table 3 shows where the programs are placed within the state agencies.

Initially, agencies establishing nongame/endangered species programs assigned the task to a biologist, sometimes one with an interest or expertise in nongame species, sometimes not. Although it is possible for a biologist to acquire the program management, public relations, and political skills to manage a new and growing program, it is not possible for any one or two people to manage multiple functions simultaneously and do them well. There have been many heroic attempts by nongame biologists to manage and promote their programs and do the technical work at the same time, but these attempts have tended to result in frustration and overwork rather than the accomplishment of high priority goals.

*T*he placement and structure of state nongame and endangered species programs are constantly changing, as if no one is quite sure what to do with them.

In the agency hierarchy, the most common placement of a nongame program is for its leader to report to the game department chief. This arrangement creates some tension if the chief is not enthusiastic about the new program. Another model is for the nongame program director to be at the same level with the person in charge of the game section, reporting to the head of a wildlife division. The highest ranking reported in the survey for a nongame program director was second in command, reporting to the agency director, in Georgia and Ohio.

There was significant upward and, oddly, downward movement of nongame personnel on the organizational charts between 1986 and 1987. Seven states appear to have promoted the nongame program leader (California, Georgia, Louisiana, Ohio, Oklahoma, Rhode Island, Texas), while in fifteen states (Arizona, Colorado, Delaware, Florida, Idaho, Indiana, Kansas, Michigan, Minnesota, Montana, North Carolina, Pennsylvania, South Dakota, Washington, West Virginia) the program leader slipped one or more notches on the totem pole (see table 3). It is difficult to interpret these results without examining the circumstances surrounding each case, but in general, running a nongame/endangered species program has not been a reliable path to upward mobility in a fish and wildlife agency.

One structure that deserves some attention is used by New York, Pennsylvania, and Colorado. The state agencies have made an effort to "integrate" game and nongame programs. The survey responses from New York and Pennsylvania did not include separate game and nongame budgets as requested. New York and Pennsylvania both have income tax check-offs that are not earmarked for nongame projects. In Pennsylvania, nongame funds are generated primarily through the sale of patches, decals, plants, and prints. Check-off funds are divided with the forestry program for plant protection.

In New York, check-off money raised through the "Return a Gift to Wildlife" program is spent on an assortment of projects, several of them infuriating conservationists. For example, some funds were reportedly used for a landowner relations program in which department personnel seek to provide access to private lands for hunting. Another project was a trapper education film. Advisory committee members appointed to make funding recommendations to the department say their suggestions are ignored. The situation stimulated a flurry of mail to the governor's office, requesting better control over the "Return a Gift" funds and specific earmarking of donations to nongame and endangered species projects. Legislation has been introduced to dedicate the funds.

Colorado's 1984 reorganization, intended to integrate game and nongame programs, resulted in nongame projects being swallowed up by the larger entity. An analysis of the program by the Wildlife Management Institute (1987) concluded that the arrangement reduced the effectiveness of the nongame program, damaged its visibility, and jeopardized its funding. The audit was carefully conducted and involved interviews with many of the department's employees. The overall conclusion was that integrating game and nongame programs may be a sound idea biologically but that administratively the nongame programs should be separate from the department's game efforts and combined with "watchable wildlife." Simply asserting that the department manages "all wildlife" does not make it so. The analysis recommended high priority for securing new sources of revenue for the nongame program.

In 1986, the New Jersey program came under fire from animal protection groups which had introduced a bill to remove the endangered species and nongame program from the Division of Fish,

Game and Wildlife and establish an equal and separate Division of Wildlife and Nongame Species. The measure was defeated, but similar proposals may surface in areas where skepticism about the motives of the fish and game agency is high.

Seventeen wildlife agencies (in Arizona, California, Idaho, Illinois, Georgia, Hawaii, Louisiana, Maryland, Massachusetts, Minnesota, Mississippi, Nebraska, North Dakota, South Carolina, Texas, Washington, and Wisconsin) have absorbed natural heritage programs established by The Nature Conservancy (see table 2). This sensible approach avoids duplication of effort and consolidates the protection of key habitats with species-oriented protection. Some states have taken over the natural heritage programs and placed them in entirely separate agencies. In Kansas, the program is under the Biological Survey at the university. Montana placed the data base in the state library. Unfortunately, effective integration of the wildlife conservation and heritage programs is more difficult when they are separated between different agencies.

Florida has taken an interesting interdisciplinary approach in which several nongame staff are placed in other departments or agencies. Four nongame staff work in the Office of Informational Services, and three urban wildlife specialists will be placed in County Extension or Institute of Food and Agricultural Sciences offices.

A final model is to separate the nongame, endangered species, and natural heritage programs entirely from the fish and wildlife agency. Mississippi, for example, consolidated all three functions under a natural history museum. Wisconsin established a Bureau of Endangered Resources with three departments: Nongame and Endangered Species, Natural Areas, and Natural Heritage Inventory. The bureau has jurisdiction over all vertebrates, invertebrates, and plants. It also has the potential to identify and begin acquiring key wildlife habitats and other natural areas.

The staffing level varies dramatically from state to state. Illinois has the highest number of staff, with 33 reported in 1987, followed by Missouri with 28, Florida with 27, Washington and California with 25 each, and Utah with 20 (see table 3).

Table 1. 1987 Sources of Funding for State Nongame (x) and Natural Heritage (•) Programs

	State—General	State—Miscellaneous	Federal—End. Species Act, Sect. 4, 6, and/or 15	Federal-Pittman-Robertson, Dingell-Johnson	Federal—Other	State Tax Check-off	License Revenues (Hunting/Fishing)	Vehicle License Plates	Trust Funds	Bonds	Interest	The Nature Conservancy	Contracts	Grants	Donations	Private/Public Matches	Sales Tax	Real Estate Tax	Sale of Items	Volunteer/In-kind Support
AL			X			X														
AK	X		X																	
AZ			X •	X •		X •	X •						X •	•	X •					
AR	•		X	X	•	X								•						
CA	X		X			X	X •		X											
CO			X	X		X	X								•					
CT	X		X																	
DE		X	X	X		X •														
FL		•					X	•							X					
GA	X •		X	X								•								
HI	X		X	X	X								•							
ID	•		X			X					X	•	X •		X				X	
IL	X •		X			X			X			•								
IN	•		X			X				X										
IA	•		X			X														
KS	•			X		X	X					•								•
KY		•	X	X	•	X	X							•						
LA		•				X														
ME			X			X					X	•	•	X •						
MD	•		X	X			X						•						X	
MA	X •		X			X •		X	X •						X					
MI			X			X				X		•	•		X				X	
MN	•		X •		X	X •			X	X		•			X	•				
MS	•		X			X	X													
MO			X			X				X							X •			
MT	•		X	X		X	X		•			•	•	X						
NE	X •		X			X									•					
NV	X •		X	X							•									
NH	•		X																	
NJ	•		X			X						•	X		X					
NY	X •		X	X		X	X		X			•								
NM	X			X		X							•	•						
NC	•	•	X		•	X							•							
ND	X •		X	X			X													
OH	•		•			X •						•	•							
OK			X			X						•	•		X					
OR	X		X		X	X						•	•	•						
PA	X •		X			X •	X						•	•	X •				X	
RI	X •		X •	X •		X •	X													X
SC	X •		X			X •												X •		
SD			X •	•	X •				X				X •							
TN	X •		X		•	X									X					X
TX	X			X				X		X			•						X	
UT	X		X			X	X								•					
VT	•				•	X	X					•								
VA	•	•	X	X		X						•	•	•						
WA	•	•	X		X •	X	X			X					X					
WV			X	X		X	•						•	•	X				X	
WI	•		X •	X	•	X •									X •					
WY			X	X	X	X				X					X	X			X	X

Funding Nongame and Endangered Species Programs

Despite the growing interest in wildlife conservation and the gradual increase in most nongame budgets, the funds continue to be derived almost exclusively from voluntary sources (see tables 1, 4, and 5). Thirty-three states had income tax checkoffs in 1987, and Maryland added one in 1988. Many states rely partially on donations or the sale of wildlife-related items. Texas, for example, initiated a stamp and print program recommended by the Audubon Council of Texas. Unfortunately, sources such as these generate insufficient and unpredictable sums, and many of the tax checkoffs have produced declining revenue. One of the main reasons for the decline in contributions is the addition of competing check-off boxes on the tax forms. Nongame contributions decreased an average of 16.4 percent when another check-off appeared on the tax form. Louisiana had seven checkoffs when the survey was conducted. The Arkansas check-off has been unusually disappointing, generating only $30,000 per year.

Many of the new sources of funding under consideration (see table 5) are also voluntary, including corporate donations, direct contributions, trust funds, and endowments.

Between 1986 and 1987, twelve states reported decreasing revenue for nongame and endangered species programs. Only Minnesota and Illinois had significantly larger budgets, attributable in part to the receipt of bond funds for land acquisition.

Many states rely at least partially on public funds. Pittman-Robertson Program funds, Section 6 money through the Endangered Species Act, and state general revenues are used to support nongame programs.

A number of states are using or considering new funding techniques. The most stable source is the 1/8-of-one-percent sales tax dedicated to wildlife conservation that was adopted by Missouri in 1976. Voters narrowly rejected a similar proposal in Arkansas. Washington state voters also defeated a sales tax increase for wildlife programs in November 1986. Florida charges new residents $4 to obtain a state vehicle registration and offers them an option of donating another dollar, all for wildlife. First-year revenue was $1.5 million. Illinois considered a general vehicle registration surcharge for motorists to mitigate wildlife mortality on the highway and compensate for general habitat destruction caused by road construction. Illinois is also evaluating a real estate transfer tax to collect a percentage of the value of each property sold. Nantucket Island in Massachusetts instituted a two percent real estate transfer tax to fund a land bank program—the first of its kind. It generates more than $80,000 per week. The goal is to preserve 15 percent of the island in open space (Klein 1986). Minnesota is establishing a one-to-one match of private funds to state revenue to acquire wildlife habitat under the "Reinvest in Minnesota" project.

Oregon conservationists introduced legislation in 1987 to tax plastics that are harmful to wildlife, dividing the funds between the Oregon Department of Fish and Wildlife and the Division of Parks and Recreation. In Connecticut, an excise tax on wildlife products was proposed, but the legislature rejected it. Other suggestions include a census tax, where each state resident pays several dollars annually to the wildlife fund, and a gross receipt tax on certain commodities, like beverages or agricultural crops. Another option is a nonrefundable deposit on beverages, selected containers, or products that are harmful to wildlife—such as plastic six-pack holders, styrofoam products, household pesticides, and fishing line.

Obviously, more funds are needed for effective wildlife conservation efforts. The survey indicated that 47 states will definitely seek federal funding under the Fish and Wildlife Conservation Act when money is available, and the other three (Florida, Missouri, and Virginia) probably will. Most respondents also indicated that their funding needs exceed current budgets. However, the amount of additional funding that nongame staff said they needed was remarkably low.

Budgets and Accounting

One important component of state wildlife programs that is absent in many agencies is a modern project accounting system for effective tracking of expenditures. It is commonly difficult to determine how much money was spent on a given project, and in many states, the program manager does not control nongame expenditures charged against the budget by staff members reporting to other administrative units. In one state, a refrigerator was charged against the nongame check-off account without the knowledge or permission of the nongame program manager. In many cases, agency staff members, even enforcement personnel in certain states, charge time against the nongame account if their work is nongame related. Such a system com-

pletely eliminates any possibility of accountability for results and generally frustrates nongame managers. It also creates a distorted picture of expenditures and leaves the door open for creative accounting schemes through which check-off or other restricted funds can be diverted to traditional programs.

Analysis of the Federal Nongame Program

Since the federal endangered species program is addressed elsewhere in this volume, the following discussion is limited to the nongame program within the U.S. Fish and Wildlife Service. The discussion is brief because the program has been strangled in recent years by an administration that seemed determined to drive the agency back into the business of producing ducks. While the level of effort devoted to endangered species has gained more attention for imperiled wildlife, the agency has not made a commitment to protecting the nation's biological diversity.

The Fish and Wildlife Service has primary jurisdiction over all 832 migratory birds. Although 654 (79 percent) of these are nongame species, 103 (12 percent) are nonhunted game species, and only 59 (7 percent) are hunted game species, 90 percent of the Service's funds still are funneled into programs related to duck hunting. Despite its own documentation of the tremendous growth in the public's interest in nonconsumptive wildlife recreation and the corresponding decline in the percentage of the population that hunts, the agency has no programs to satisfy the viewing public.

In the late 1970s, the Fish and Wildlife Service initiated a program entitled "Unique Wildlife Ecosystems," conducting an extensive inventory of the wildlife communities in need of protection. If

the program had not been abandoned, considerable progress might have been made in acquiring some of the high priority lands for the National Wildlife Refuge System. A few of the areas have been protected, often through private efforts, others have been developed, and, for most, the status is unknown.

The nongame program is housed in the Office of Migratory Bird Management. In 1983, Fish and Wildlife Service biologists drafted the Nongame Migratory Bird Management Plan, outlining a strategy for the identification of nongame birds thought to be declining and proposing specific actions to improve the survival chances for 28 species of birds known to be in trouble. The plan represented a modest, though respectable, effort to begin looking seriously at factors known to be detrimental to birds and included a proposed staff expansion designed to place at least one nongame biologist in each of the regional offices. Unfortunately, the plan was buried and forgotten until resurrected by conservation groups, which lobbied successfully for modest funding through the congressional appropriations process. Most of the funds have been allocated to research conducted at the Patuxent Wildlife Research Center in Maryland, and very little of the money has been allocated to projects in the field.

Conclusions and Recommendations

Growth and change are inevitable as the fledgling nongame programs mature. Changing public expectations and a new administration offer new opportunities for shaping both state and federal nongame programs. But an opportunistic approach to wildlife conservation is not enough. Nongame programs at the state and federal level need coordinated long-range plans if we are to achieve the goal of protecting the natural abun-

dance and diversity of wildlife.

Defenders of Wildlife and other conservation organizations have been active in efforts to support and improve the existing state and federal nongame and endangered species programs and to secure additional funding for the agencies involved in resource protection efforts. However, in these times of fiscal austerity, it is impossible to secure new revenue sources—or significantly increase appropriations from traditional sources—without providing a solid plan for spending the money. Tangible program benefits are essential. Even if the resources to implement the plans are not now available, it is important to specify how the resources would be used. Without such plans, funding is unlikely to materialize.

Coordinated Nongame Program Plans

Defenders of Wildlife recommends that the appropriate state and federal agencies develop and implement coordinated nongame program plans incorporating the components outlined below.

Research. The highest priority research needs should be determined in these four categories: (1) sociological studies to identify the constituency for wildlife conservation outside the traditional core of consumptive users and to determine what this constituency expects from the agencies; (2) studies based on existing information to identify the habitats in greatest need of protection and to develop a short-term priority acquisition list; (3) studies to save critically endangered species, emphasizing information gaps relevant to the development of recovery plans; and (4) studies of wildlife mortality factors known to have significant adverse impacts with the objective of documenting, then minimizing, those impacts.

It is important to balance the need for research against the need for immediate action to reverse the decline of species already in trouble. Whether the studies are conducted by the agency or under contract with universities or other outside parties should be decided on the basis of benefits, costs, timing, and reliability of the researcher. Every research project should have a specific goal, directly relevant to the program's statutory mandate. The results and management implications should be published in popular journals to enlist public support for conservation programs.

Habitat Conservation. Two fundamental changes are crucial in the planning for habitat conservation, in addition to the obvious need for more money. The first is an interagency approach to locate and conserve the most ecologically significant habitats. Approaching this important task piece by piece, according to bureaucratic divisions of land, is counterproductive. The second change needed is to extend the planning horizon from an annual or biennial cycle to fifty or more years, then concentrate on conserving the most critically endangered habitats first.

Once such habitat conservation planning is underway, a strategy can be developed to use existing sources of money and various cooperative agreements to protect habitat. For example, federal funds are available under the Land and Water Conservation Act to purchase lands for federal refuges, parks, forests, or other conservation areas. Direct grants to the states can also be obtained through this fund to acquire parks, wildlife areas, or other preserves. Private funds may be available from land trusts or through local citizen groups, sometimes with corporate sponsorship. Conservation easements can be negotiated with local governments or individuals, sometimes with tax benefits for the landowners. Bond issues are another avenue for obtaining funds from state, city, or county governments. The possibilities are numerous, but without identification of the wildlife areas in greatest need of protection, citizen efforts are not likely to be focused on those areas.

Recovery of Endangered Species and Habitats. With limited dollars available, it is essential to target the money effectively toward the most serious problems, requiring managers to make difficult decisions. At the risk of oversimplifying the situation, it seems reasonable to weigh the chances of success against the probable cost of a given effort. Efforts to protect endangered habitats may provide more long-term benefits than extraordinarily expensive captive-breeding programs for a single species with only a few individuals remaining. The widely held perception that the public supports projects involving just a few highly visible species should not drive recovery priorities.

Nonconsumptive Wildlife Recreation. The increasing level of participation in wildlife-oriented recreation, particularly viewing, photography, bird feeding, and related activities, is of tremendous significance for conservation, since these participants have an obvious interest in maintaining wildlife populations. In order to meet the demand for nonconsumptive uses in the future, it is important to quantify this demand and determine what kind of facilities will be needed to meet it. It is also important to determine the economic impact of this increasingly popular form of recreation and to develop funding strategies for the future. If the economic benefits are clear, especially to the tourist industry, investments in the resource will be easier to obtain through political channels.

Education and Interpretation. Recent surveys generally indicate a high level of interest in wildlife, particularly among urban residents. Demographic trends suggest that urbanites will become increasingly influential in making decisions as the population continues to shift away from rural areas. High quality interpretive displays and printed information, carefully targeted to those with an interest in viewing, photography, and other nonconsumptive activities, cannot help but generate support for habitat conservation. The most important factor is to determine a specific goal for any educational effort to utilize resources most effectively.

New Constituency and Funding Base. It may take a number of years under the best of conditions to establish a new constituency and funding base for the conservation of natural diversity and the provision of a wide range of "appreciative" use opportunities. The transition will be painful and rough without careful planning and the allocation of appropriate resources. Unless qualified persons are assigned to the task of defining what the program should be like in ten or fifteen years and authorized to develop and implement a strategy for making it happen, agencies will continue to be driven by external events that are certain to hamper their effectiveness in conserving resources.

Meeting the Challenges of the 1990s

In the next decade, state and federal efforts to reverse the decline of endangered wildlife and to prevent additional species from becoming endangered are likely to change substantially in response to a number of factors. The most significant pressure will come from the environmental community seeking more effective, ecosystem-based conservation programs; from the nonconsumptive wildlife recreationist seeking equal attention from the wildlife agencies; and from scientists developing sophisticated new technologies for defining essential habitats. The changes are already beginning to occur, offering exciting opportunities for resource agency administrators to enhance their ability to

Nongame programs at the state and federal level need coordinated long-range plans if we are to achieve the goal of protecting the natural abundance and diversity of wildlife.

meet the expectations of the public.

The recommendations that follow are primarily for agency administrators and legislators, since most are beyond the scope of nongame and endangered species program managers to implement.

Evolving Goals

Wildlife management in the next decade will, in responsive agencies, enter a new phase in its evolutionary process. The trend is for ecologists to consider the entire spectrum of species, place less emphasis on the introducion of exotics, and work to restore native wildlife and plant communities where they have been disrupted (Henderson 1987). Paralleling this trend, wildlife managers will place more emphasis on identifying the attitudes, expectations, values, and needs of resource "users" and other publics and incorporating this feedback into programs.

In short, important goals in the future will be to protect the integrity of wildlife communities and to provide a broad spectrum of recreational opportunities.

Agency Structure

The traditional division of wildlife species into categories like game, nongame, sensitive, state listed, federally listed, and so on seems to work against a comprehensive system of ecosystem protection. In the long run, responsibility for the protection of all wildlife—including plants, vertebrates and invertebrates, and both terrestrial and aquatic species—should be consolidated. However, any agency needs functional divisions to administer different programs, and efforts to integrate game and nongame programs have so far proved premature. There is already so much variation from one state agency to the next that it is unrealistic to propose one structure that will work in every case. Nevertheless, emerging patterns suggest that certain functions cluster conveniently to facilitate effective conservation practices and to appeal to the new constituencies most likely to provide long-term political and financial support for fish and wildlife agencies.

One possibility is to establish a new division with a name like "Division of Ecosystem Conservation," responsible for maintaining viable native wildlife communities with a minimum of manipulation. The division chief would need a resource background and strong planning, administrative, and political skills. The position should be at an equal level with the game division and fish division heads, reporting to the agency director. This new arrangement might include several distinct functions or departments:

1) restoring endangered habitats and populations, concentrating on the implementation of habitat-based recovery plans rather than on listing activities;

2) preventing the endangerment of wildlife communities by monitoring habitats, species, and adverse impacts on populations and by taking affirmative steps to establish a system of preserves to ensure the continued viability of all major habitat types;

3) creating and maintaining natural heritage or equivalent data bases that consolidate inventories of lands and species;

4) acquiring natural areas, concentrating on the highest priority lands; and

5) developing wildlife appreciation programs to answer the demand for nonconsumptive wildlife recreation and related nature studies, including educational efforts and the provision of facilities for enjoyment of the resources (the department handling this function would also provide public relations support for the division).

As previously mentioned, there are any number of organizational schemes that can be effectively utilized if agency directors provide adequate support and enthusiastic leadership for the program. There is no substitute for good management, in which qualified employees are assigned to accomplish high-priority goals and rewarded appropriately. The system must effectively distinguish between activity and results.

Public Relations

The approach an agency takes in dealing with the outside world is extremely important. How the agency is perceived will determine, in the long run, whether it will be effective in accomplishing its goals. Communications specialists observe that ninety percent of perception is reality. Therefore, to change perception, one must ultimately change reality.

If a traditional fish and game agency director intentionally keeps a small nongame program ineffective and short on resources, the strategy will not escape the notice of the public. This can be expected to affect adversely contributions to the tax check-off or voluntary funding schemes in the short run and to hinder the cultivation of a new constituency in the long run.

A fish and wildlife agency must carefully balance the commitment to activities that are necessary to protect the resource against the expectations of the public. In the ideal world, resource conservation and recreation are compatible, but conflicts are inevitable. How the agency handles such conflicts is the essence of a public relations program.

Public meetings, although better than no public involvement at all, do not really demonstrate the "will of the people." They attract a small group of highly committed, sometimes extreme, often dissatisfied citizens—an unrepresentative cross-section. Advisory committees, although sometimes helpful, do not represent the public either.

In order to find out what the public wants, carefully controlled surveys, administered periodically by professionals capable of accurately interpreting the results, should be conducted by every fish and wildlife agency. The Responsive Management Project sponsored by the Western Association of Fish and Wildlife Agencies has been developed in computer modules specifically for this purpose.

Several state fish and wildlife agencies, including those in California, Oregon, Kansas, Texas, Florida, Arizona, Colorado, and Utah, have sponsored such surveys. The data tend to confirm a wide gap between the public's expectations and agency programs. The gap is especially large between the level of interest in nonconsumptive wildlife recreation and the level of effort devoted to programs intended to meet the demand. Another consistent gap is between the level of interest in and awareness of nongame and endangered species programs and the relative amounts of money allocated to them.

As an important part of the public relations strategy, eliminating the terms "nongame" and "nonconsumptive use" from program titles and developing more appealing and understandable descriptive terms would be very helpful.

Funding for Ecosystem Conservation

A reliable and substantial funding source is essential to all ecosystem conservation programs. At the federal level, a minimum of $100 million dollars annually from excise taxes, severance taxes, or the general fund is needed to implement the Fish and Wildlife Conservation Act of 1980. The passage of the proposed American Heritage Trust Act would establish a secure source of revenue for land acquisition.

After defining the federal role in the conservation of wildlife communities, additional staff and funding will be required. The most likely source is the federal appropriations process, allocating money from the general treasury.

Each state should conduct a thorough analysis of long-term funding needs, recognizing that new, stable funding will be essential to the establishment of effective programs to prevent further decline in the nation's wildlife resources. Voluntary funding mechanisms, like a semi-postal stamp and state tax check-offs, should be considered, if at all, only to supplement more substantial and reliable sources of funds.

Based on analysis of the funding patterns that have emerged to date and on the successes and failures in securing new revenue sources, Defenders of Wildlife offers the following observations.
• Virtually every survey of public preferences for various funding options reveals two things. First, the public is highly supportive of government

> *A reliable and substantial funding source is essential to all ecosystem conservation programs.*

efforts to conserve wildlife, and second, nearly everyone expects someone else to pay.
• "User fees," while somewhat attractive politically, are generally resisted by the industries or groups expected to pay the bills. There are other problems with user fees. The logistical and administrative costs associated with their collection often exceed the anticipated revenue. This problem is especially intense in sparsely populated areas, often the places with high wildlife values. Another obvious difficulty is identifying the "user." It is helpful to make a distinction between programs with recreation goals and those focused on conservation. It is legitimate and appropriate to charge access fees to individuals using areas with trails, viewing blinds, parking, restrooms, and other facilities. It is less defensible to expect the viewing public to foot the entire bill for conservation programs designed to protect the state's natural heritage. Like clean water and air, ensuring overall environmental quality is everyone's responsibility and should be financed from general revenue.
• Mitigation fees offer tremendous potential that has not been tapped effectively for wildlife conservation except for the adoption of real estate transfer taxes in a number of states. Generally, the funds are allocated to natural areas programs. Mitigation fees are based on the assumption that certain activities cause harm to wildlife but are necessary to support human society. Therefore, a fee is assessed to compensate for the damage, and the funds are dedicated to the acquisition or restoration of habitat. It is highly appropriate for these fees to be used for conservation, and they should form a major percentage of the new revenue for ecosystem protection.

• General funds, while attractive, are always difficult to obtain because of the competition from other worthy causes. However, this source is usually favored by the public.

• The most important concept in securing new funds is that nobody is likely to approve a major expenditure unless there is an outstanding justification for it. The habitat acquisition bonds approved by voters in California, Maine, New York, Illinois, and Minnesota were successful because land purchase is a tangible benefit. The sales tax increases proposed in Washington and Arkansas may have failed because people were not generally in support of giving bureaucracies more funds for unspecified purposes, particularly more staff.

• One pattern that characterizes recent successful efforts is a broad coalition of support for a wide range of related purposes. In California, the 1988 bond will purchase parks, coastal areas, and wildlife habitat. New York's bond addressed the cleanup of hazardous materials. "Something for everybody" helps build the political support necessary for passage of such bonds.

• Finally, there is a trend toward increasing overlap between the public and private sectors, both in funding sources and activities. Public agencies seeking new funds have explored corporate and foundation grants with limited success. Those sources are suitable for specific projects but are not likely ever to supply a significant or dependable source of money for agency programs.

Educating Managers of the Future

As the more progressive and responsible fish and wildlife agency directors struggle with the logistics of implementing more responsive and ecologically oriented programs, it is painfully obvious that the limiting factor is often the availability of qualified staff. Perhaps the resource manager of the past could stay in the woods with the birds and mammals, but the manager of the future must have solid interdisciplinary training to protect natural resources effectively from an endless and intensifying series of destructive activities. Specifically, program directors need well-developed political, interpersonal, and communications skills in addition to management expertise.

Sociologists, ecologists, and conservation biologists are desperately needed to manage the transition from single-species management for consumptive users to the conservation of entire biological communities for future generations. Few, if any, universities currently offer such an interdisciplinary degree.

Protecting Habitats for Biological Diversity

In the last decade, nongame programs have grown from virtual nonentities in many states to well-established and fully accepted programs in at least a few fish and wildlife agencies. The next decade will present the opportunity for even more significant change. The necessary transition will require agencies to abandon the assumption that they exist exclusively to raise certain wildlife species for hunters and to adopt the concept of ecosystem protection with all native species of plants and animals valued as important components. Hunting and fishing may still be important, but habitat protection must be the essential goal. This goal can never be realized without a financial commitment from a large segment of the population. Ted Williams (1986) shares this conclusion:

> Whether we admit it or not, we are a part of the biota and our health depends on the health of the other parts. Why should those working to protect the biota pay extra while those working to destroy it pay nothing? Why not a wildlife-habitat tax to be levied on, say, developers who build shopping malls in swamps and thereby deprive the rest of us of wildlife habitat? At the very least wildlife management should be underwritten by everyone. . . . Those who think it important to work within the present system certainly have the right to their opinion. They have the right simply to keep checking off the nongame square on their tax forms, to keep sending in their bird club dues, to keep setting up bluebird nesting boxes, to keep out of the way. What they do not have the right to do is complain about the lack of wildlife.

With the 1980s coming to a close and a new federal administration assuming responsibility for a number of natural resource programs, new opportunities for shaping these programs and their state equivalents will surface. But, as stated earlier, an opportunistic approach to wildlife conservation is not enough. It is time to define a new reality, to make the commitment—including the financial commitment—to do what is needed to preserve biological diversity by stanching the decline of our native wildlife and protecting the integrity of natural communities.

Sara E. Vickerman, regional program director for Defenders of Wildlife, operates out of the Northwest regional office in Portland, Oregon. She holds her M.S. degree in environmental science from Southern Oregon State College and her B.S. in anthropology from California State University. She has conducted several wildlife appreciation surveys and has pioneered the idea of increasing tourism and support for wildlife conservation by developing and marketing wildlife viewing opportunities, including the 1988 publication of a wildlife viewing guide for the State of Oregon.

Selected Bibliography

Broadway, M. No date. Attitudes towards nongame wildlife: A survey of Kansas residents. Unpublished report. Kansas Fish and Game Commission, Topeka.

Coggins, L. 1975. Legal protection for marine mammals: An overview of innovative resource conservation legislation. *Environmental Law* 6: 1.

Greenberg, L.B. 1985. An evaluation of alternative mechanisms for financing nongame management in Arizona. Unpublished (M.S. thesis). University of Arizona, Tucson.

Henderson, C.L. 1987. Past and future perspectives for nongame wildlife conservation. Unpublished report. Minnesota Department of Natural Resources, St. Paul.

Klein, W.R. 1986. Nantucket tithes for open space. American Planning Association. *Planning* 52 (August): 10-13.

Naisbitt, J. 1982. Megatrends: Ten new directions transforming our lives. Warner Books, New York, New York.

Rawlings, M.S., and L.A. Neel. 1987. Unique and important wildlife habitat investigation. Nevada Department of Wildlife, Reno.

Tetreault, F. 1986. Buying back our heritage. *Outdoor Highlights* 14 (June): 11.

U.S. Fish and Wildlife Service. 1982. National survey of fishing, hunting, and wildlife-associated recreation. U.S. Department of the Interior, Washington, D.C.

Vickerman, S. 1987. Nongame checkoffs—only the beginning. *Endangered Species Update* 4 (November): 1-4.

Wildlife Management Institute. 1987. Colorado's nongame fish and wildlife efforts: Organization, funding and program needs—A report to the Director and Wildlife Commission. Colorado Department of Natural Resources, Denver.

Williams, T. 1986. Who's managing the wildlife managers? *Orion Nature Quarterly* (Autumn): 16-23.

Appendix: Tabular Summaries of State Survey Data

Table 2. Nongame and Endangered Species Programs by State for 1987

(1986 data, if different from 1987, is included in brackets.)

	Nongame Plan	Status Survey NG/ES	Fish and Wildlife Agency Jurisdiction: Plants	Invertebrates	NG/ES Habitat Acquisition	Number of Sites for Nongame	Number of Acres for Nongame	Agency Affiliation of Heritage Program
AL	No	Few [Some]	No	?	Insuffic. $ [No]	0	0	No Natural Heritage data base [Seeking private funding]
AK	No	Few [No]	No (Dept. of Nat. Resources)	M/C	No [Some]	0	0	No Natural Heritage Program [Vetoed by governor]
AZ	Yes [No]	Some	No (Agric. Commission)	M/C	Potential [Beginning]	1	100	Game and Fish Dept.
AR	No	Some T/E	No (NH)	Yes	No $, some donated [Yes]			Natural Heritage Commission
CA	No [Start]	Some NG, Most T/E	Yes (T/E)	T/E, M/C	Yes	75	150,000	Dept. of Fish & Game, NG Heritage Section
CO	No	Some NG, All T/E	No (Natural Areas, DNR)	M/C	Potential [Some]	0	0	Dept. of Natural Resources, Div. of Parks and Recreation
CT	No	Some	No (State Geological Nat. History Survey) [Federal T/E program]	Yes	No	0	0	Dept. of Environmental Protection, Geological and Nat. History Survey
DE	Yes	Some	No (Div. of Parks & Rec.)	Yes	No [Some]	0	0	DNR, Div. of Parks and Recreation and Dept. of Nat. Resources and Environmental Control
FL	Yes	Some	No (Dept. of Ag. & Cons. Serv.)	M/C	No [Yes]	FL has several land acquisition programs		Nature Conservancy contract through Dept. of Nat. Resources
GA	Yes	Some [Many]	Yes	Yes [Potential]	Yes	0	0	Dept. of Nat. Resources, Game and Fish Division
HI	Yes	Many [Some]	Yes	Yes	Yes, insuff.$ [No]	9 (+ 36 off-shore sites)	80,000	Nature Conservancy contract with Div. of Forestry and Wildlife
ID	Yes	Some T/E	No (Dept. of Parks and Rec.)	Yes	Insuff. $	0	0	Fish and Game Dept.
IL	Yes	Some T/E	T/E	T/E M/C	Yes	18	1,412	Dept. of Conservation, Div. of Nat. Heritage
IN	Yes [No]	Some	No (Div. of Nature Preserves)	M/C	Yes	2	150	DNR, Div. of Nature Preserves
IA	Yes [Start]	Some [Yes]	No (Bur. of Preserves & Eco. Serv.)	T/E	Yes [Some]	3	187	DNR, Bureau of Preserves and Eco. Services
KS	Yes [Started]	Some	No	T/E, M/C	Potential [No]	0	0	Biological Survey, Univ. of Kansas, and The Nature Conservancy
KY	Yes	Many [Started]	No (Dept. of Ag.–ginseng only)	Yes	Yes, insuff. $	0	0	Nature Preserves Commission

NG = Nongame
ES = Endangered Species

T/E = Threatened and Endangered Species
M/C = Mollusks and Crustaceans

DNR = Department of Natural Resources
NH = Natural Heritage Program

	Nongame Plan	Status Survey NG/ES	Fish and Wildlife Agency Jurisdiction: Plants	Invertebrates	NG/ES Habitat Acquisition	Number of Sites for Nongame	Number of Acres for Nongame	Agency Affiliation of Heritage Program
LA	Yes [No]	Few [No]	No (Dept. of Ag.)	M/C	Insuff. $	0	0	Dept. of Fisheries and Wildlife and Dept. of Nat. Resources
ME	No [Start]	Some	No	T/E, M/C [Yes]	Yes [Potential]	0	0	The Nature Conservancy
MD	Yes	Some	NH	NH	No	0	0	Dept. of Nat. Resources–Forest, Park, and Wildlife Service
MA	Yes	Many	Yes	Yes	Yes	4	236	Div. of Fisheries and Wildlife
MI	No	Few, T/E [T/E]	Yes	T/E M/C	Yes, no NG $ [No]	thousands of acres		Dept. of Nat. Resources, Div. of Wildlife
MN	Yes	Many, T/E [T/E]	T/E	M/C,T/E, butterflies [M/C]	Yes	4	1,454	Dept. of Nat. Resources, Wildlife Section
MS	No	Some T/E [T/E]	Maybe T/E [No]	Yes	Potential	1	593	Museum of Nat. Science, Dept. of Wildlife Conservation
MO	No	Yes	Yes	Yes	Yes	105	17,864	Dept. of Conservation
MT	No	Some NG, All T/E	No	M/C	No, potential under different program	1	150	Montana State Library
NE	No	Some [T/E]	T/E	T/E, M/C [T/E]	Potential, insuff. $	0	0	Game and Parks Commission
NV	No	Many T/E	No (Forestry)	Yes [No]	Potential [No]	0	0	State Parks and The Nature Conservancy
NH	No	T/E [Audubon]	No (Dept. of Res. and Eco. Development)	Yes	Insuff.$ [No]	0	0	Dept. of Resources and Economic Development
NJ	No	Some [T/E+]	No (Office of Nat. Lands Mgmt.) [TNC]	Yes	Some	1	400	Dept. of Environmental Protection, Div. of Parks and Forestry
NM	Yes	Some NG, Many T/E [T/E]	No (State Parks) [Nat.Res.Dept.]	M/C	Potential [Some]	1	20	Dept. of Energy, Minerals, and Natural Resources
NY	ES	Many [Few]	No (Div. of Lands and Forests)	Some [Yes]	T/E [Some]	0	0	The Nature Conservancy and Dept. of Environmental Conservation
NC	1989	Few T/E	No (Dept. of Ag.)	T/E ? M/C [T/E]	Yes [Some]	0	0	Dept. of Nat. Resources, Div. of Parks and Recreation
ND	1988	Some	No (Parks & Rec.)	Yes	Potential [No]	several sites managed for all wildlife		Game and Fish Dept., Natural Resource Section
OH	No	Some	No (Div. of Nat. Areas & Preserves)	Yes	Potential [Some]	0	0	Dept. of Natural Resources, Div. of Natural Areas and Preserves
OK	No	Some	No	Yes	Yes [No]	2		Biological Survey, Univ. of Oklahoma
OR	Yes	Some	No (Dept. of Ag.)	No [aquatic]	Yes, insuff.$ [Some]	4	300	Div. of State Lands and The Nature Conservancy

NG = Nongame   T/E = Threatened and Endangered Species   DNR = Department of Natural Resources
ES = Endangered Species   M/C = Mollusks and Crustaceans   NH = Natural Heritage Program

	Nongame Plan	Status Survey NG/ES	Fish and Wildlife Agency Jurisdiction: Plants	Invertebrates	NG/ES Habitat Acquisition	Number of Sites for Nongame	Number of Acres for Nongame	Agency Affiliation of Heritage Program
PA	No	Many	No (Dept. of Env. Res.)	No (Fish Commission)	Potential	several sites managed for all wildlife		Dept. of Environmental Resources and The Nature Conservancy
RI	No	Many [Some]	T/E	Yes [No]	Potential	0	0	Dept. of Environmental Mgmt., Div. of Planning and Development
SC	No	Yes [Some T/E]	T/E(habitat acquisition only)	T/E [No]	Yes [Some]	15	2,000	Wildlife and Marine Resources Dept.
SD	No	T/E	T/E [Yes]	T/E [No]	Insuff. $	several sites managed for all wildlife		Game, Fish and Parks Dept.
TN	Yes	Some T/E	No (Dept. of Conserv., Eco.Serv.Div.)	M/C	Insuff.$ [Yes]	1	5	Dept. of Conservation, Div. of Eco. Services/Regional Natural Heritage Project: TVA
TX	No	Some [T/E]	Yes	Yes	Potential	0	0	Parks and Wildlife Dept.
UT	Started	Some	No	Crayfish and brine shrimp	Potential [Some]	1	7.4	Dept. of Natural Resources (pending)
VT	No	Few	No [Yes]	Yes	Yes [Potential]	0	0	Dept. of Natural Resources
VA	No	Many	No (Dept of Ag.)	Yes [Potential]	Yes, insuff. $	0	0	Dept. of Conservation and Historic Resources
WA	Yes	Some	No (Dept. of Nat. Res.)	Yes	Potential	13	4,567	Dept. of Natural Resources and Dept. of Wildlife
WV	No [Yes]	Few NG T/E	T/E (Dept. of Ag.–ginseng only)	Yes [Partial]	Insuff. $	1	33	Dept. of Natural Resources
WI	No	Many [Some]	Yes	Yes [Nat. Areas]	Yes	2	2	Dept. of Natural Resources, Endangered Resources Bureau
WY	Yes	Many [Some]	No (Dept. of Ag.)	No	Potential [No]	0	0	No longer has a formal Heritage Program (was in Dept. of Environmenal Quality)

NG = Nongame
ES = Endangered Species

T/E = Threatened and Endangered Species
M/C = Mollusks and Crustaceans

DNR = Department of Natural Resources
NH = Natural Heritage Program

Table 3. Nongame and Endangered Species Program Organization by State for 1987
(1986 data, if different from 1987, is included in brackets.)

	Total NG/ES staff (FTE)	Regional NG staff	Outside research contracts	Natural Heritage FTE staff: Perm.	Temp.	Total	Title of NG/ES leader	Immediate supervisor position relative to agency director (1st)	Ranking
AL	4 [4.5]	1	Yes	0	0	0	Program Coordinator, Nongame Wildlife	Chief of Wildlife	4th
AK	3.33	4 [No]	Yes	0	0	0	Coordinator, NG Wildlife Program	Deputy Director Game Division	3rd
AZ	10	6 w/other responsibilities [Other]	Yes	8	7	15	NG Branch Supervisor and ES Coordinator	Chief of Wildlife Management	4th
AR	2	0	Yes	10	1	11	Chief-ES, NG, Urban Wildlife Section	Chief-Federal Coordination and Support Serv. Div.	4th
CA	25 [14]	5+ [Other]	Yes	5	9	14	Chief-NG Heritage Sec [Coordinator-NG, Birds and Mammals]	Dep. Dir. for Wildlife [Chief - Wildlife Mgmt.]	3rd [4th]
CO	4	0	Yes	3	0	3	2 Program Specialists: Aquatic and Terrestrial	State Wildlife Managers	3rd/4th [2nd]
CT	2	0	Yes [No]				Nonharvested Program Biologist [NG/ES Coordinator]	Supervisor of Wildlife Research	4th
DE	1.5	Other	Yes	2	0	2	NG/ES Coordinator	Research Biologist Supervisor [Wildlife Administrator]	5th [3rd]
FL	27 [20]	12 [5]	Yes	7	5	12	NG Section Supervisor	Asst. Director, Div. of Wildlife [Director]	5th [2nd]
GA	2 FTE 2 PTE [2.75]	0	Yes [No]	1	4	5	Deputy Commissioner for Programs [Sr. Wildlife Biologist]	Dept. of Natural Resources Commissioner [Asst. Chief, Game Mgmt.]	2nd [4th]
HI	11	0	Yes	10	3	13	Wildlife Program Manager	Administrator, Div. of Forestry and Wildlife	3rd
ID	3 [1]	0	Yes	2	1	3	State NG Wildlife Manager	Chief, Bur. of Wildlife	4th [3rd]
IL	33 [32]	16 [11]	Yes	1	1	2	Chief-Natural Heritage Division	Director-Office of Natural Resource Management	3rd
IN	2	2	Yes	4	2	6	Environmental Unit Supervisor	Chief of Wildlife	3rd
IA	4 [4.3]	0	Yes	5	0	5	NG Wildlife Biologist [Research Superintendent]	Wildlife Research Supervisor	5th [4th]
KS	2	1 [Other]	Yes	3	2	5	Project Leader-NG and Endangered Wildlife [Urban Biologist]	Wildlife Program Admin. [Species Mgmt. Supervisor]	5th in 1988 [4th]
KY	3 [2]	0	Yes	5	3.5	8.5	NG Wildlife Program Coordinator	Director, Wildlife Div.	3rd
LA	1 [2-3]	0 [Other]	Yes [No]	4	1	5	NG Wildlife Program Coordinator [Upland Game Study Leader]	Upland Game Study Leader [Research Study Leader]	6th [7th]

NG=Nongame	FTE=Full-time Employees	TVA=Tennessee Valley Authority
ES=Endangered Species	PTE=Part-time Employees	TNC=The Nature Conservancy

	Total NG/ES staff (FTE)	Regional NG staff	Outside research contracts	Natural Heritage FTE staff: Perm.	Temp.	Total	Title of NG/ES leader	Immediate supervisor position relative to agency director (1st)	Ranking
ME	2 [0]	Other	Yes	2.5	0	2.5	Project Leader-ES and NG Wildlife	Wildlife Research Section Supervisor [Director of Research]	6th
MD	1	Other	Yes	7	14	21	NG and ES Program Manager	Assoc. Dir. of Wildlife	3rd
MA	4 [10]	0 [Other]	Yes	10	1+	11+	Director-Nat. Heritage & ES; Asst. Director-Div. of Fisheries and Wildlife	Deputy Director for Administration, Div. of Fisheries and Wildlife	3rd
MI	3.2 [4.1]	0	Yes	5	2-10	7+	NG, ES Program Coordinator [Forest, Wildlife, NG Supervisor]	Section Chief-Farm, Urban Wildlife [Chief-Wildlife Div.]	5th [4th]
MN	9 [8]	5	Yes	4	5	9	NG Wildlife Supervisor	Program Manager-Wildlife Sec. [Chief - Wildlife Section]	4th [3rd]
MS	5	0	Yes	3	(+1 contract)	4	Nat. Heritage Coordinator	Museum Director	4th
MO	28 [25]	3 [Yes]	Yes	4	3	7	Nat. History Administrator	Assistant Director	3rd
MT	2.59 [2]	0.17 [Other]	Yes	4	1 (+2 seasonal, contract)	5+	Nongame Coordinator Wildlife Division [Nongame Biologist]	Mgmt. Bureau Chief,	5th
NE	4	1	Yes	3	0	3	Nongame Specialist	Chief, Wildlife Div.	4th
NV	4.75 [4]	4 [3]	Yes	3	0	3	NG Staff Biologist	Chief, Game Div.	3rd
NH	0	0	No [Yes]	0	2(state) 1(TNC)	3	Federal Aid Coordinator[Biologist]	Chief, Game Division [Chief, Game Mgmt. and Research]	3rd
NJ	11	8 [12]	Yes	4	0	4	Bureau Chief-Office of ES and NG	Asst. Director-Div. of Fish and Game	3rd
NM	5	0	Yes	2	0	2	Asst. Div. Chief of Biological Services for ES	Chief-Biological Services Division	4th
NY	[11]	1	Yes	4	1	5	[Supervising Wildlife Biologist, NG Unit Leader & Research Scientist, ES]	[Species Section Head]	[4th]
NC	6	3 [4]	Yes	4	2	6	NG Section Manager Management	Chief-Div. of Wildlife	4th [3rd]
ND	1	0	Yes	4	1	5	Natural Resource-Zoologist	Natural Resource Program Coordinator	3rd
OH	3+	Other	Yes	8	14 PTE	13 PTE	Chief, Div. of Wildlife [Asst. Admin.-Fish and Wild. Mgmt. and Research]	Director, Dept. of Nat. Resources [Exec. Admin.-Wildlife Mgmt. and Research]	2nd [4th]
OK	2	0	Yes	1	0	1	NG Wildlife Biologist	Federal Aid and Research Coordinator	3rd [5th]
OR	7.33 [7]	5 PTE [6]	Yes	3	2-3	5-6	NG Program Coordinator	Asst. Chief-Wildlife Div.	4th

NG=Nongame
ES=Endangered Species

FTE=Full-time Employees
PTE=Part-time Employees

TVA=Tennessee Valley Authority
TNC=The Nature Conservancy

	Total NG/ES staff (FTE)	Regional NG staff	Outside research contracts	Natural Heritage FTE staff: Perm.	Temp.	Total	Title of NG/ES leader	Immediate supervisor position relative to agency director (1st)	Ranking
PA	0.25 --- ---	0 FTE (many PTE) --- 0	Yes (West) (East) Yes Yes	1.5 4	1.5 1	3 5	1. Protected Wildlife and ES Coordinator 2. Botanist 3. Herpetology and ES Coordinator	Director, Bureau of Game Management Chief, Fisheries Mgmt. Unit	3rd [2nd] 4th
RI	1-2	0	No	2	1	3	Sr. Natural Resource Specialist	Deputy Chief-Wildlife Div.	3rd [4th]
SC	9 [8]	3.5	Yes	14	7	21	Chief-NG Heritage Trust Program	Director-Div. of Wildlife and Freshwater Fisheries	3rd
SD	2.1 [1]	0.1 [0]	Yes	Same as NG			Wildlife Biologist	Chief-Planning	5th [4th]
TN	3+ [3]	4 PTE	Yes	TN: 8 TVA: 4	1 0	9 4	NG and ES Coordinator	Chiefs of Fisheries and Wildlife	4th
TX	6	4 [Other]	Yes	8	1	9	Program Director-Migratory Birds, NG, and ES	Director- Wildlife Div. [Prog. Dir.-Migratory Birds, NG, & ES]	3rd [4th]
UT	20 [18]	5	Yes	0	0	0	Chief-NG Section	Asst. Director-Field Programs	3rd
VT	2.5 (1988) [1.5]	0	Yes	2	1	3	Asst. Director (1987), NG Project Leader (1988)	Director of Wildlife (1987), Asst. Director (1988)	3rd 3rd
VA	1 [3]	0	Yes	4	0	4	Project Leader-Wildlife Biologist	Asst. Chief of Game	5th
WA	25 (31.6 budgeted for 1987-89) [18]	11 [7]	Yes	5	3	8	Manager, NG Program	Chief, Wildlife Mgmt. Div.	4th [3rd]
WV	3.5 [6]	0 [Other]	Yes	3-4	2	5-6	Wildlife Biologist II [Leader, NG Unit]	Asst. Chief of Special Projects	5th [4th]
WI	6 [1]	0	Yes	9.5	3	12.5+	Chief-NG Section	Director-Bureau of Endangered Resources	3rd
WY	3	Other-28 @ 1/12 time (2 in 1987)	Yes	0	0	0	Nongame Coordinator	Supervisor of Biological Services	4th

NG=Nongame   FTE=Full-time Employees   TVA=Tennessee Valley Authority
ES=Endangered Species   PTE=Part-time Employees   TNC=The Nature Conservancy

Table 4. Nongame and Endangered Species Program Funding by State for 1987 [1986]: Part 1
(Figures in thousands of dollars)

	Nongame/Endangered Species Budget		Total Fish and Wildlife Agency Budget	Percent of Total Budget to Nongame	1987 Natural Heritage Program Budget Appropriated from Legislature (including acquisition)
	1987	[1986]			
AL	97	[122]	11-12,000	0.9	0
AK	244	[269.5]	10,000	2.5	0
AZ	551	[500]	19,000	2.9	406*
AR	112	[125]	20,000	0.5	290*
CA	17,000	[15,100]	110,000	15.4	1,224*
CO	800	[1,000]	35,700	2.2	105*
CT	152	[130]	825	18.4	
DE	57	[42]	3,500	1.6	31*
FL	1,512	[1,500]	35,041	4.3	259*
GA	100	[140]	19,400	0.5	150*
HI	243	[306]	4,010	6.0	250*
ID	243	[92]	21,700	1.1	0*
IL	3,486	[1,400]	137,803	2.5	3,486* (Division of Nat. Heritage)
IN	179	[305]	9,750	1.8	146*
IA	204	[133]	14,500	1.4	225
KS	523	[489]	12,491	4.1	0*
KY	100	[110]	17,000	0.59	228*
LA	75	[75]	35,000	0.21	0*
ME	200	[125]	15,000	1.3	0*
MD	135	[125]	3,200	4.2	1,337*
MA	576	[297]	5,776	9.9	191*
MI	700	[600]	11,940	6.0	154*
MN	1,278	[684]			405*
MS	375	[535]	16,455	2.2	87
MO	2,500	[2,500]	84,204	2.9	90*
MT	176	[203]	31,700	0.5	132*
NE	285	[250]	24,253	1.2	0*
NV	210	[210]	12,000	1.7	0*
NH	17	[0]	5,931	0.29	73
NJ	525	[450]	10,000	5.2	0*
NM	368	[460]	12,401 (incl. "Share with Wildlife" Program)	3.0	0*
NY	---	[1,331]	---	---	0*
NC	348	[200]	20,557	1.6	160*
ND	50	[50]	---	1.1	100

* Natural Heritage Program has additional sources of funding (see Table 1).

	Nongame/Endangered Species Budget		Total Fish and Wildlife Agency Budget	Percent of Total Budget to Nongame	1987 Natural Heritage Program Budget Appropriated from Legislature (including acquisition)
	1987	[1986]			
OH	625	[350]	18,000	3.4	319*
OK	162	[133]	17,874	0.9	0*
OR	494	[517]	53,000	0.9	0*
PA	---	[691]	---	---	East: 0* West: 40*
RI	74	[44]	2,947	2.5	0*
SC	635 (incl. Herit.)	[300]	30,000	2.1	150*
SD	65	[50]	9,714	0.7	same as nongame budget
TN	282	[225]	20,000	1.4	350*
TX	180	[178]	99,535	0.18	240*
UT	778	[711]	16,000	4.8	0*
VT	---	[50]	---	---	0*
VA	600	[600]	20,000	3.0	0*
WA	1,086	[800]	28,302	3.8	1,600*
WV	204	[115]	21,300 (7,600 Wildlife Division)	0.95	0*
WI	300	[200]	291,000 (all Dept. of Natural Resources programs)	0.1	108*
WY		[668]			0

* Natural Heritage Program has additional sources of funding (see Table 1).

Table 5. State Nongame and Endangered Species Program Funding by State for 1987: Part 2

	1987 Nongame/Endangered Species Program Funding Sources and Corresponding Amounts		Funding Sources Considered	Check-off Revenue 1986	1987
AL	Tax check-off Pittman-Robertson	62,000 45,000-90,000	Nongame endowment. Corporate donations. Prints, stamps.	↑	↑
AK	General fund Endangered Species Act Section 6	244,200 27,000	Check-off on permanent fund dividends. Gifts.	Not available.	
AZ	Check-off Pittman-Robertson ESA Section 6 ESA Section 4 Donations, contracts License revenue	294,000 57,000 96,000 14,000 35,000 55,000	1/8 of 1 percent sales tax for wildlife, Missouri Plan. General fund.	↓	↑
AR	ESA Section 6 License revenue Pittman-Robertson	48,800 28,680 35,250	General sales tax.		↑
CA	Check-off Personal license plates General fund ESA Section 6 Bonds	850,000 11,000,000 3,000,000 350,000 2,000,000	More state general funds. Nonconsumptive user fees.	↓	↑
CO	Check-off (not all to nongame) Pittman-Robertson/Dingell-Johnson ESA Section 6 (incl. some check-off $) License revenue	407,000 164,448 119,699 ?	Department seeking to diversify wildlife funding. Marketing study in 1987.	↓	↑
CT	General wildlife bureau budget ESA Section 6	148,000 4,000	Print and stamp sales.	Not available.	
DE	Check-off Pittman-Robertson ESA Section 6 Coastal Zone Management funds	26,000 2,500 10,000 18,630	Corporate donations. General fund.	↓	↓
FL	License plate fee ($4—new residents) Vehicle regis. renewal ($1 contribution) Donations	2,036,832 157,138 1,741	None.	Not available.	
GA	General fund Pittman-Robertson ESA Section 6	45,000 20,000 35,000	Voluntary contribution program (Nongame Fund). Habitat acquisition bond.	Not available.	
HI	General fund Pittman-Robertson ESA Section 6 U.S. Fish and Wildlife Service	66,669 67,500 132,507 12,000	Tax check-off. Private funding. Habitat stamp (50% game, 50% nongame).	Not available.	
ID	Check-off (FY86) ESA Section 6 Interest Sale of items Donations Contracts	68,602 123,000 8,000 2,500 2,000 4,000	ESA Section 4. Pittman-Robertson. License revenue. Prints.	↓	↑
IL	General fund Check-off Bonds ESA Section 6 (reimbursement)	1,181,100 305,000 2,000,000 25,135	Surcharge on vehicle license plates. Real estate transfer tax.	↓	↑

	1987 Nongame/Endangered Species Program Funding Sources and Corresponding Amounts		Funding Sources Considered	Check-off Revenue 1986	1987
IN	Check-off	432,000	None.	↑	↑
	ESA Section 6	undetermined			
	Interest	undetermined			
IA	Check-off	171,000	None.	↑	↔
	ESA Section 6	25,000			
	ESA Section 15	16,000			
KS	Check-off	137,306	State general fund.	↔	↑
	License revenue	125,585			
	Pittman-Robertson	250,775			
	ESA Section 6	123,000			
	Dingell-Johnson	9,260			
KY	Check-off	44,500	None.	↑	↔
	Pittman-Robertson	50,000			
	License revenue	6,000			
	ESA Section 6 (not incl. in program budget)	62,000			
LA	Check-off (fiscal year 1986)	23,000	None.	↑	↓
ME	Check-off	115,000	State general fund.	↓	↓
	ESA Section 6	55,000			
	Interest	6,000			
	Grants	25,000			
MD	License revenue	12,000	Instant lottery game.	Not available.	
	Pittman-Robertson	84,000	Corporate donations.		
	ESA Section 6	25,000	Added check-off in 1988.		
	Sale of items	14,000			
MA	Check-off	295,308	Corporate gifts.	↓	↑
	Bonds	175,000	Interest income.		
	General fund	106,041			
	ESA Section 6	18,400			
	Donations	500			
	Trust fund	10,000			
MI	Check-off	660,000	Trust fund. General fund.	↑	↑
	ESA Section 6	200,000	Pittman-Robertson funds.		
	Interest	60,000			
	Sale of items	18,000			
MN	Check-off	800,000	"Reinvest in Minnesota," 1:1 state matching fund for capital investments—approved.	↑	↔
	Bonds	64,000			
	ESA Section 6	78,000			
	Interest	62,000			
	Donations	10,000			
	Combined Federal Campaign	4,000			
MS	Check-off	51,000	Donations.	↑	↓
	License revenue	300,000			
	ESA Section 6	23,900			
MO	Sales tax	8,191,509	None.	Not available.	
	Pittman-Robertson, Dingell-Johnson, Wallop-Breaux	7,030,288	(Figures are for total wildlife budget— nongame not separate.)		
	License revenue	15,051,431			
	Interest	896,645			
MT	Check-off	41,246	None.	↔	↓
	Pittman-Robertson	9,081			
	ESA Section 6	124,000			
	License revenue	1,883			
	Grants	?			

	1987 Nongame/Endangered Species Funding Sources and Corresponding Amounts		Funding Sources Considered	Check-off Revenue 1986	1987
NE	Check-off General fund ESA Section 6 (doesn't add to budget but replaces $ spent from general fund, check-off)	156,002 128,689 27,500	None.	←→	↑
NV	General fund Pittman-Robertson ESA Section 6 (if approved)	52,500 157,500 15,000	Gifts. Grants. Conservation groups.	Not available.	
NH	ESA Section 6	16,500	Requests from legislature.	Not available.	
NJ	Check-off ESA Section 6 Donations Contracts	488,000 7,000 10,000 20,000	Prints. Stamps. Real estate transfer tax. 1:1 matching check-off with state general fund.	↑	↓
NY	Check-off ESA Section 6 Pittman-Robertson Dingell-Johnson General fund License revenue Acquisition bonds	1,500,000 13,600 } unable to separate nongame	Investigating new revenue sources for entire department.	Not available.	
NM	Check-off ("Share with Wildlife") General fund Pittman-Robertson, Dingell-Johnson	121,500 60,900 186,000	None.	↑	↓
NC	Check-off ESA Section 6	381,030 26,400	Nongame Advisory Committee.	↑	↑
ND	General fund Pittman-Robertson License revenue ESA Section 6	 limited 40,000	Income tax check-off passed for 1988 tax year.	Not available.	
OH	Check-off	625,000	None.	↑	↑
OK	Check-off ESA Section 6 Contributions	134,000 32,000 undetermined	Real estate transfer tax.	↓	↓
OR	Check-off General fund ESA Section 6 Marine Mammal Protection Act Sect. 109	227,338 195,860 46,000 25,000	Tax on soft drinks, plastic, bottles. General fund in 1988-89.	↓	↓
PA	*Wildlife:* Check-off State general fund License revenue ESA Section 6 Sale of items Grants *Plants:* Check-off *Fish:* Check-off License revenue	 94,000 ? 300,000 35,000 250,000 40,000 150,000 124,468 ?	Land & Water Conservation Fund. Coastal Zone Management. General fund for Heritage Program.	↓	↑
RI	Check-off General fund Pittman-Robertson ESA Section 6 License revenue In-kind volunteer services	24,563 3,000 34,893 2,700 1,500 7,431	Donations.	New.	

	1987 Nongame/Endangered Species Program Funding Sources and Corresponding Amounts		Check-off Revenue Funding Sources Considered	1986	1987
SC	Check-off	200,000	None.	←→	←→
	General fund	385,000			
	ESA Section 6	50,000			
	Document stamp tax (Heritage Trust)	1,300,000			
SD	License revenue	5,000	Several new ideas.		Not available.
	ESA Section 6	30,000			
	Army Corps of Engineers	25,000			
	Contracts	5,000			
TN	General fund	100,000	State payroll tax with income tax check-off. Sale of art prints. Citizen committee to review funding options.		Not available.
	License revenue	110,133			
	ESA Section 6	63,000			
	Foundations	7,200			
	In-kind volunteer services	1,667			
TX	Agency funds	?	ESA Section 6.		Not available.
	Sale of items	42,000			
	Pittman-Robertson	131,007			
	Interest	10,000			
	Game, Fish, and Water Safety Fund	45,000			
UT	Check-off	175,000	None.	↑	↓
	General fund	272,352			
	ESA Section 6	203,680			
	License revenue	126,909			
VT	Check-off (unspent)	96,000	Contribution line on license application. Lottery related to above. Stamp, print sales.		New.
	License revenue	60,000			
VA	Check-off	600,000	Lottery. Property transfer tax. Sales tax.	↑	↑
	Pittman-Robertson	200,000			
	ESA Section 6	20,000			
WA	Personal license plates	697,076	Possible fee increase for personal license plates. General fund (not specified for nongame).		Not available.
	License revenue	?			
	ESA Section 6	25,994			
	Interest	39,588			
	Donations	2,992			
	Forest Service	74,046			
	National Marine Fisheries and U.S. Fish and Wildlife Service	89,403			
WV	Check-off	50,107	General fund. Corporate donations. Endowment fund. Sales tax.	↓	↓
	Dingell-Johnson	17,500			
	ESA Section 6	41,500			
	Sale of items	107,524			
	Donations	1,538			
WI	Check-off	160,000	None.	↑	↑
	Pittman-Robertson	40,000			
	ESA Section 6	58,000			
	Donations	45,000			
WY	ESA Section 6	?			Not available.
	Donations	?			
	Matching funds	?			
	Dingell-Johnson, Pittman-Robertson	?			
	Other federal funds	?			
	License revenues	?			
	Sale of items	?			
	Interest	?			
	In-kind volunteer services	?			